*How to be
Safe
in an
Unsafe
World*

How to be Safe in an Unsafe World

Donald D. Gilbert

Robinson Township Library
606 N. Jefferson
Robinson, IL 62454

COPYRIGHT © 1984 BY
HORIZON PUBLISHERS & DISTRIBUTORS, INC.

All rights reserved. Reproduction in whole or any
parts thereof in any form or by any media without
written permission is prohibited.

International Standard Book Number
0-88290-235-0

Library of Congress Catalog Card Number
84-80450

Horizon Publishers Catalog and Order Number
4051

Printed and Distributed in the
United States of America
by

**Horizon
Publishers &
Distributors, Inc.**

50 South 500 West
P.O. Box 490
Bountiful, Utah 84010

CONTENTS

Chapter One
INTRODUCTION TO HARD TIMES 11

Chapter Two
RESIDENTIAL SECURITY 14
Crime Avoidance in the Home 15
The Lived-In Home While You're Away 16
    Lighting 16
    Automatic Security Lighting 16
    Sound Like You're Home 17
Doors 17
    Door Locks 19
    Sliding Glass Doors 20
    Padlocks and Hasps 24
    Keyless Locks 25
    Key Control 26
Windows 26
    Double-Hung Windows 27
    Sliding Windows 28
    Hinged Windows 28
Cooperative Construction 29
    Shrubs and Trees 29
    Fencing 29
    Roofing 30
Guard Dogs 30
Alarm Systems 32
    Control Panels 32
    Input Sensors 33
    Area Sensors 34
Alarm Signals 36
    Police Department Alarm 36
    Central Station Alarm 36
    Proprietary Alarm 37
    Local Alarms 37

Choosing an Alarm 38
Choosing an Alarm Company 39
Constructing Hiding Places 40
    Baseboard Vault 41
    Cedar Chest in the Floor 42
Neighborhood Security 44
    Steering Committee 44
    Neighborhood Passive Watch 45
    Alarm Procedures 46
Timing 46

Chapter Three

PERSONAL PROTECTION 48
Crime Avoidance 49
Professional Defenses 52
    Self-Confidence 52
    Physical Fitness 53
    Personal Combat Skills 53
    CS and CN Gas 53
        Gas Tactics 53
    Guns 54
        Which Gun 55

Chapter Four

SECURITY IN HARD TIMES 57
The Steering Committee 57
Police 58
Active Patrol 59
Closed Security System 61
    Gates 61
    Guardhouse 63
Communications 63
Active Defense 64
Observation Points 65
Windows 65
Porches 67
Education of Others 67
Timing for Hard Times 68
Apartment Complexes 69
    Fencing 69
    Closed Security System for Apartments 70

Chapter Five

RURAL OR FARM SECURITY 71
Ultimate Security 72
Farm Communication. 75
Perimeter Security. 76
    Fencing 76
    Gates 77
Wall Defense Positions. 77
Home Construction. 78
Alarm System 78
Community Roadblocks. 78
Tactics 79

Chapter Six

ORGANIZATIONAL SECURITY 81
Church Security. 82
Alternative Lifestyle 82
The Food Cache. 84

Chapter Seven

RETAIL STORES. 85
Security of the Future 85
Security Booth. 87

Chapter Eight

GAS STATIONS. 89
Decor 89
Service Station Construction 90
    Inside Functions 90
Company Policy 92

Chapter Nine

INTERNAL THEFT PREVENTION AND DETECTION. 94
You've Made Your Own Bed 94
Applicant Screening 95
All There Is Left. 97
Personal Screening of the Job Applicant. 97
Application for Employment 98
Use the Professionals 98
    The Polygraph and the Applicant 99
    Periodic Polygraph Examinations 100

Background Investigations 101
Inventory Control 102
Video Recorders 102
Undercover Operatives 102
Shopping Service 103

Appendix A—Recommended Books on Financial Planning
   for Hard Times....................................... 105

Appendix B—Recommended Books on Physical Independence
   for Hard Times....................................... 107

Index... 109

Chapter One

INTRODUCTION TO HARD TIMES

Over the past several years, in order to become more responsible for my family's needs, I have made it my business to read many books on investments and economics. I have also attended many seminars on the subject of economics. I received from this education a pretty grim picture of our future. Authors and instructors have presented pictures of our society breaking down as it becomes more involved in a projected inflationary spiral. Some authors have offered projections that start with inflation that gets progressively worse until it becomes a complete collapse or a massive depression. Other authors offer a scenario that drops the economy into a massive depression with all its ramifications.

After what was to be several years of intensive study on my part, I found that one issue stood out: many authors stated that they felt crime and criminal behavior would be on the rise during this projected period of time; none offered any indication as to the extent of the problem or how to cope with it.

Because I deal with crime and theft on a regular basis within my own business, I decided to look into it myself. I wanted to know if there were books or studies available on security which were written specifically for hard times. I was unable to find a real book on security for hard times except those that offer, as a first line of defense, a big gun. It seemed that everyone who ever contemplated getting along in hard times always went from point "A" to point "X" skipping "B, C, D, E" and never offering alternatives that might prevent violence and aggressive behavior.

My objective then became quite clear: to present an alternative to people in this country who believe that troubled times are ahead; an alternative that would not require the use of violence as a means of protection except as a last resort.

Over the last fifteen years I, as a security consultant and investigator, have been involved with all types of criminals. Men and women have confessed to me that they have committed rape, murder, incest, theft, child beating, and every other kind of crime imaginable. I have personally caused several of those people to go to jail. Unfortunately a very small percentage of people who commit crimes actually go to jail.

The frequency of crimes of this type is on the increase. Drug abuse is up ... crime is up ... taxes are up ... government spending is up! So let me ask you—what are the chances for a stable, growing economy?

Over the last several months it has come to my attention that there has been a marked increase in the sales of guns. Sporting goods stores have been selling more and more of the specialty gun called the "Riot Shot Gun." I can only believe that when people are confronted with an inner feeling of insecurity, brought about by unstable times, they will react instinctively to protect themselves. If the guns are purchased only by those who recognize the signs of the times, there are a lot of people who feel that our society is heading for trouble. One thing is clear: there are many people who, when faced with troubled times, have only one resource available to them—their guns. They have no other means for establishing the kind of security they require.

I have not written the foregoing paragraphs to teach you economics; I am not an economist. Nor do I want to teach you history; I am not a historian. I am a security consultant and have been for fifteen years. I have studied our social and economic situations and I have come to certain conclusions:

> I believe that our society is about to become involved in one of the most unrestful periods in American history. Whether the unrest arises from hyperinflation, from depression or from birth pains prior to the Tribulation—Americans will have to cope with a new and hostile environment. This environment will be controlled by a small segment of the population who, when confronted with shortages in the basic necessities such as food and other material goods, will react according to their violent natures. When such people are confronted with shortages they take what they need or want.
>
> I, along with any number of people, believe that these problems will surface in many forms of violence: crime rates will increase as much as 200 percent; riots will occur; irrational panic behavior brought about by the shortage of necessities will occur.
>
> The growth of police departments will not keep up with our need for protection. In fact, police departments may have very serious problems of their own. Take, for example, a police department in a small town during an inflationary period. If this town, during a period of one year, suffered (along with the rest of society) from an inflation rate of 35 percent, there would be an increase of 25 to 35 percent in their city government costs. Most cities receive a good portion of their income through sales tax revenue. When inflation hits, the consumer will be

hard pressed to maintain a standard of living and will decrease spending on all but essential items. The consumer will concentrate on food purchases and debt reduction, leaving new purchases in a depressed state. The small town will not only have a decrease in sales tax revenue —they will have a hard time collecting any tax needed to pay the wages of emergency-service personnel.

In the following chapters are suggestions for personal protection that require direction, hard work, cooperation, and community involvement. By arming yourself with knowledge rather than with guns, you may be able to confront the hard times ahead with a minimum of violence. I simply believe that when hard times come, people should be capable of defending themselves, but that guns and violence should be used only as the very last resource.

Chapter Two

RESIDENTIAL SECURITY

Burglary is one of the biggest growth industries in America today. The typical burglar has considered its impressive advantages. There is no employer—no one to hire or fire him. There is a minimal capital investment: screw driver, bolt cutters, and a few other inexpensive tools. The industry has a high rate of return: $526 per job is the national average (The Sourcebook of Criminal Justice Statistics—1981). The burglar has a naive customer, one who seldom offers resistance to his sales objective. There is little resistance. (Police departments can't watch homes. We are fortunate if they can look at a neighborhood once a day.) Neighbors who are afraid of meddling offer little deterrence. The working hours are short—a few during the day or early evening.

Considering such working conditions, I'm surprised that more people are not employed in the age-old profession of burglary. Can you imagine how nice it would be to be in a business where there is at least one residence on every block where the occupant is going to buy a product that will have an average sales commission of $526? The word is finally out—this great profession has caught on and the number of its employees is increasing every year.

Only once in thousands of entries does a burglar choose a home where he knows someone is present. Most burglars pursue their trade because they can steal with a minimum risk of aggressive contact. They provide themselves with opportunities least likely to involve any confrontation. Quite often burglars are known by their victims: neighborhood kids or local drug addicts.

A typical burglar will drive through a likely neighborhood and look for obvious signs of emptiness or accessibility:

1. No lights on in the evening or, if they are on, a quick check shows that lighted rooms are vacant.
2. No sounds from the dwelling.
3. An open, empty garage.

4. House or garage doors left open.
5. An unkept lawn.
6. Newspapers or mail delivered but not taken in.
7. Large shrubs to hide behind so the burglar can get a closer look or gain access.
8. Dark yards offer the criminal an opportunity to get closer to the house. If there are hedges on both sides, so much the better. At least those neighbors can't become involved.

Burglary is not some mysterious crime performed only by heroin addicts, deranged maniacs, or people possessed by the devil. It only requires someone who can handle a little bit of excitement and who believes that he deserves whatever he steals.

As unemployment rises and money gets tighter many more men will hold their families together with a few burglaries on the side. In fact, while doing pre-employment screening for some clients, I have spoken with many men who use burglary as a means of stability in their economic lives. If the rent gets behind or the kids need school clothes they do one or two jobs to tide them over. This is the easy crime. Just walk up to an empty home, go in, and take what you want.

Actually it's just about that easy. The police do prosecute some burglars but the volume of burglaries makes prosecution difficult. In 1978 there were 3,104,500 burglaries (The Sourcebook of Criminal Justice Statistics — 1981) in the United States. In addition, there were 5,983,400 larceny-thefts, 991,600 motor vehicle thefts, and a grand total of 10,079,500 property crimes — a 60 percent increase in property crimes since 1968. Only 15 percent of all burglaries are actually followed by arrest of the burglars. Of these, a very small percentage are ever sent to jail. It seems that burglary is no more hazardous than driving down a busy street.

CRIME AVOIDANCE IN THE HOME

Our primary concern, in this chapter, is to establish the absolute baseline for security in a home environment. Whether you live in an apartment or out in the country, you must maintain as many of the basic security requirements as possible.

First, and probably most important, is to appear secure. Obviously Fort Knox could be broken into by two platoons of Marines and the proper equipment, but it has not been done because the Fort looks so formidable. Your residence has to appear secure and show an outward appearance of nonaccessibility without drawing undue attention.

Second, the perimeter must be secured in a way that prevents all but the most extreme entry measures.

Third, your security measures must not draw attention to your *individual* home. They must not announce to the casual observer that your house has something valuable inside. Don't let your home stand out from those of your neighbors.

My objective is to suggest that you use the three elements just listed in your security system.

THE LIVED-IN HOME WHILE YOU'RE AWAY

The first objective in any plan to discourage burglary is to make your home appear as though someone is always there. It doesn't matter that burglars know people do this. If a burgular has to guess whether someone is in the house he generally won't bother breaking in. Why should he? There is bound to be another house down the street where he doesn't have to guess.

Lighting

Outside lights should be used to expose any unwanted entry into your property. Ideally, two 60-watt bulbs in front and two in back should be used in conjunction with a timer that will turn them on at dusk and off at sunrise. The lights should be placed close to the borders of your property, perhaps on light posts or fencing. These lights deter burglars by exposing them to your view or at least giving them the feeling of exposure. Burglars don't want to be seen. They love hiding places and dark corners.

Inside your house should be at least two timers that activate at least two lights in separate rooms while you are away. The best plan is to have both lights turn on at dusk and then have them alternate turning off and on throughout the evening until your normal bedtime. Place one light in a room with a window facing toward the street. This must be a room that normally has the curtains drawn at all times during the evening. A front bedroom will do if you do not usually leave the bedroom curtains open during this time. The thief must not be able to look into the rooms and discover that they are empty. Put the timing device on your windows permanently.

Light timers can be purchased for under $20. Some sell for as little as $6. The best timer has a twenty-four-hour clock and the capacity to turn on and off three or four times in an evening.

Automatic Security Lighting

One attractive deterrence device is a simple automatic light switch that is activated by a person's presence. The sensor switch is a passive infrared sensor that detects the temperature difference between the background wall (air temperature, and so on) and the target (person, auto) as the target moves through the field of the sensor. Upon sensing a presence it turns on a light—or lights—outside the house. When the burglar approaches the front door—or any other area covered by such a sensor switch—the lights are automatically turned on. The burglar would most likely believe that he had been discovered. And even if he knew or suspected that the device was there, he is now exposed.

With this sensor you may save on electricity. Further, you can avoid tripping over the garden hose and those steps.

The sensor has several drawbacks: animals and high winds that move shrubs and bushes may cause false alarms. Most sensors have a sensitivity adjustment to account for random motion but care must be taken to not disarm the sensor by a too high sensitivity setting.

I believe any device that announces a presence on the outside of a home in advance of any aggressive activity is worth its weight in gold. The security light control can be enhanced by the addition of a low volume buzzer connected to the same circuit as the light. Now, not only do the lights go on but the buzzer goes off in the house announcing a presence outside the house.

Sound Like You're Home

If you were to walk up to the outside of your home or apartment during the day or night and listen at the window, what would you hear? More than likely you wouldn't hear much noise from the people who are home; you are more likely to hear the radio or TV playing in the background. If you stood there for three or four minutes and heard nothing you would probably think no one was at home. That's exactly what a burglar would think.

While you are away for a few days an inexpensive timer works well to give the sound of background noise when no one is home. The timer can be plugged into the radio or TV and can be set to go on and off during the day and stay on in the evening until your normal bedtime. You could avoid the use of the timer entirely and leave the radio on all the time. Or you could make it a practice to turn on a radio every time you leave the house. Transistor radios draw very little current from an electrical outlet.

Dogs are a fearsome thing to a burglar. Just don't scold them when they bark as someone approaches your house. Most dogs' natural tendency will be to bark at an intruder. When your dog barks tell him he's a good dog. (The training of a dog as a watchdog is covered in a later chapter.)

DOORS

Our early ancestors designed their dwellings to shelter themselves from the weather and to protect them from wild animals and bad people. As centuries went by, wild animals and criminals became less and less of a concern. Now, however—even though we are not bothered by animals—we have to design our otherwise decorative homes with protection in mind. A front door with a beautiful stained glass window offers little resistance to a burglar. The window can simply be broken, or cut, allowing the burglar to reach in and open the door.

A good, protective door should be built of wood at least one-and-three-quarter-inches thick. This door should have a minimum of three hinges with the hinges facing the inside of the house. Each hinge should be held in place by three-inch screws set into the door and frame.

Wide-angle viewers should be installed in every external door at eye level. The better-quality viewer costs less than $10 and is made of solid brass. It has a 190-degree viewing area and fits most door sizes.

190° DOOR VIEWERS

BRASS OR CHROME

Door viewers like the one pictured here are a must. No one should ever open their door unless they are willing to let the person who is on the outside inside. After you open the door it's too late to decide that you don't want anything to do with that visitor.

Use of an intercom is also a good idea. A visitor can be questioned briefly before the door is unlocked.

If the hinges on your door are on the outside, install nonremovable hinge pins. If you have an external door with the hinges on the outside, a simple trick will protect you until you can replace the hinges: remove the center screw in each of the hinges and replace one screw with a pin that protrudes about three-eighths inch, leaving the other screw hole empty. When the door

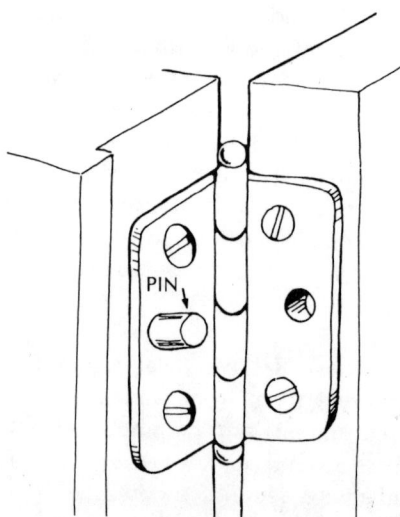

is closed the pin fits in the opposite hole. If the hinges are removed the door will still be held in place by the pins and your regular locking devices.

Glass doors pose special problems. If you have a decorative glass panel in a door that you do not want to give up, try installing a security screen or decorative wrought-iron grill that can withstand several extreme blows from a large hammer. Use nonremovable bolts on the outside to hold the security screen or wrought-iron in place.

The ultimate external door is a metal one at least a quarter of an inch thick. Either an existing wooden door can be encased or the door can be hollow and filled with a foam for insulation. There are commercial companies that sell a door made of 18-gauge metal specifically designed for homes. Metal doors do become costly though—some run as high as $800. When you consider the improvement of external doors, you should include all doors that can be reached from the outside, including the garage door.

Your garage door could be a big problem. Most locking devices available for garages use a barrel bolt or a lock and hasp. In both cases there is a considerable amount of metal exposed to the outside of the garage. Bolt cutters can, in most cases, be used to cut these items and gain entry. When buying hasps or barrel bolts get them in hardened steel.

While it is difficult to lock a garage from the exterior it is reasonably easy to lock it from within. If you have a pedestrian door to your garage or an entrance from the house your problems are simplified. Now your bolts and hasps are on the inside and easily protected from damage. Use a dead bolt with a one-inch throw in the pedestrian door.

Door Locks

In many homes the front door is secured with a latch lock without a plunger in the doorknob. A latch without a plunger can easily be opened with a credit card or a sharp screwdriver. A burglar just inserts his instrument into the crack, pushes the plunger, and the door opens.

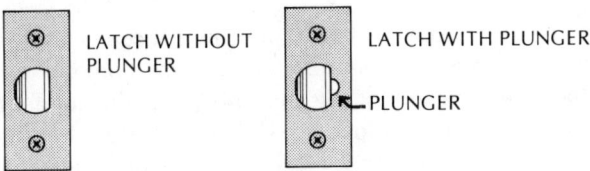

A key-in-the-knob locking device with a plunger in the latch offers some protection against manipulation from a credit card or screwdriver, but it must not be considered an effective security measure. If this device is your only protection it can be effectively disarmed with a large, sharpened screwdriver or crowbar. The burglar simply has to insert the large screwdriver into a crack close to the lock and pry the door outward. In most cases the door is wrenched out of place as the latch is forced away from the strike plate.

A chain lock is just as unsecure. It is usually installed by several half-inch screws with one or two set in the door and one or two in the door frame.

One swift kick by a hundred-pound juvenile is enough to tear the chain latch from the door frame, perhaps taking some molding with it. It is far better to not use a device that gives you a false sense of security.

The locking device I recommend is the deadbolt lock used in conjunction with a regular door lock. The deadbolt should have a one-inch throw of case-hardened steel with the connection screws holding the lock together on the inside of the door. Screws used on the strike plate should be three inches long or long enough to reach the structural member within the wall. (See Figure 1.) There are larger reinforced strike plates, nine inches long, that use four 3-inch screws and two smaller screws that strengthen its very vulnerable point. (See Figure 2.) The cylinder that surrounds the locking mechanism must be tapered and free-moving to prevent wrenching of the locking mechanism. The deadbolt lock should be unlocked with a key on the outside and with a turn of the thumb on the inside. Homeowners should avoid the double-cylinder deadbolt lock that requires a key to open both sides. First, if a fire or other emergency occurs precious minutes might be lost in searching for the key. Second, many people find that using a key to lock their door every time they enter is a tiresome chore and they soon abandon the practice which leaves them with little or no protection.

Some people leave their keys in the lock on the inside when they get home, but when your house has two or three doors that require these locks the hazard of abandoning the practice is still present.

Special precautions must be taken when there is a window in the door or one within forty-five inches of the locking device. Metal grating or wrought-iron grates should be designed with bars every one to two inches to prevent hands from reaching through to the inside of the door. (See Figure 3.)

Sliding Glass Doors

Sliding glass doors are a modern invention usually used in warmer climates to bring as much of the outdoors into the home as possible. Unfortunately, they are designed for the convenience of the builder and repairman, not for security. Burglars love the sliding glass door because it offers very little resistance. One reason it offers little resistance is because manufacturers don't build the window into the frame; they tip the window into a frame which has already been installed. This allows the owner to easily replace the window if it breaks by simply lifting the window up and out of the bottom track, then tipping it out and down until it clears the upper track. Simple. The problem is that it's just as simple for a burglar to tip the window out as it is for the owner. A burglar just inserts a screwdriver under the door at the bottom and lifts up.

There are many ways to reinforce your sliding glass doors but the simplest way is as follows:

Fig. 1

CYLINDER DEADLOCK: The deadbolt is locked or unlocked from the exterior with a key and from the interior with a turn-piece. *Never lock yourself in your home.* This lock features a new solid steel security shield and thicker high security strike plate with extra-long screws, a one-inch dead bolt, heat-treated steel insert which turns with any attempted cutting, a tapered all-steel cylinder guard that revolves to resist attempted wrenching, and two ¼-inch-diameter heavy-duty bolts. (Courtesy of Kwikset, Division of Emhart Industries Inc.)

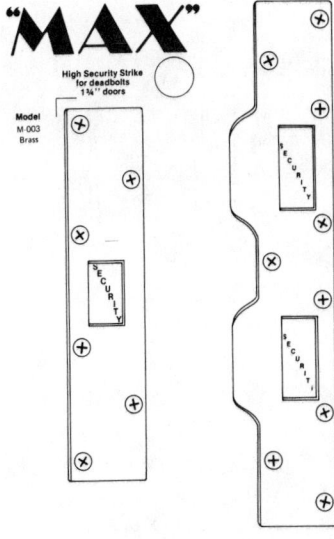

Fig. 2

MAX: This could be the answer for the weakest point in any locking device. These strike plates are a hundred times stronger than the standard deadbolt strike. By using 3-inch screws you have effectively tapped into the strength of your 2-by-4-inch main frame. (Courtesy of BLC Products)

Fig. 3

PROTECTO-LOK: This locking device has the standard advantages of a good deadbolt lock set with the additional advantage that it can be opened from the inside by simply turning the knob. This one action retracts the deadbolt as well as the deadlocking latch. (Courtesy of Kwikset, Division of Emhart Industries, Inc.)

In the center of the upper track, drill at least four holes spread evenly through the track groove. Insert a roundhead screw in each of these holes and tighten them down until the window, while sliding through the track, just barely clears the screws. When properly installed the screws will prevent anyone from removing the sliding glass door by lifting up on the window until the screws are removed from the inside.

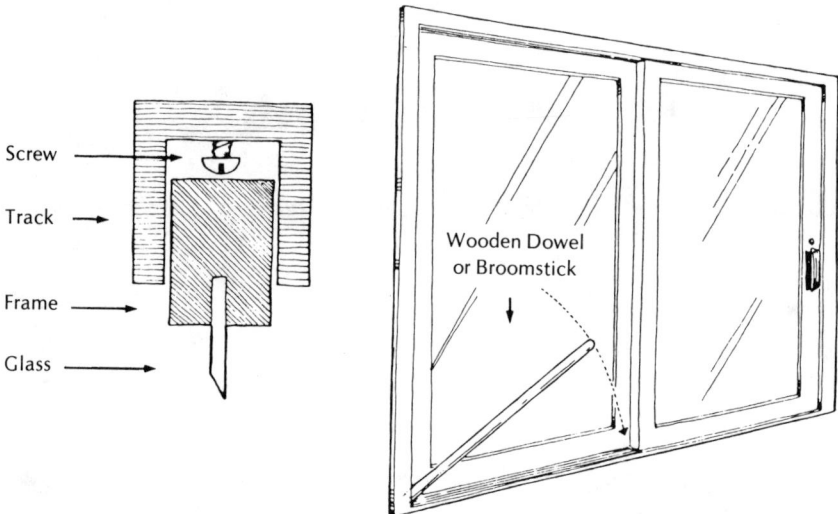

Cut a dowel or broom handle to fit snugly in the part of the bottom track that is exposed after the glass door has been closed.

These dowels have, upon occasion, been wrenched out of position by the use of a long, slender instrument such as a screwdriver or ice pick which has been inserted between the windows to lift the dowel or broom handle out of its groove. This can be prevented by obtaining a piece of metal about two and a half inches wide and two feet long and at least a quarter of an inch thick, with three or four holes drilled in it for inserting screws. This plate should be attached to the back side of the sliding door so that when the door is closed the plate fits snugly to the opposite window frame and effectively eliminates easy access to the dowel.

A third precaution is to drill two holes through the top track which enters the upper window frame on an angle downward toward the outside. This is done with the door closed. Be careful not to drill all the way through the window frame. Insert an eyebolt in each hole to effectively hold the window frame in place. Attach a string or small chain to the eyebolt and fix the other end of the string or chain to a screw in the window molding to hold the eyebolt when it is removed. Avoid the use of nails or other items that you cannot attach in some way. If the nail becomes lost the procedure may soon be discarded.

RESIDENTIAL SECURITY

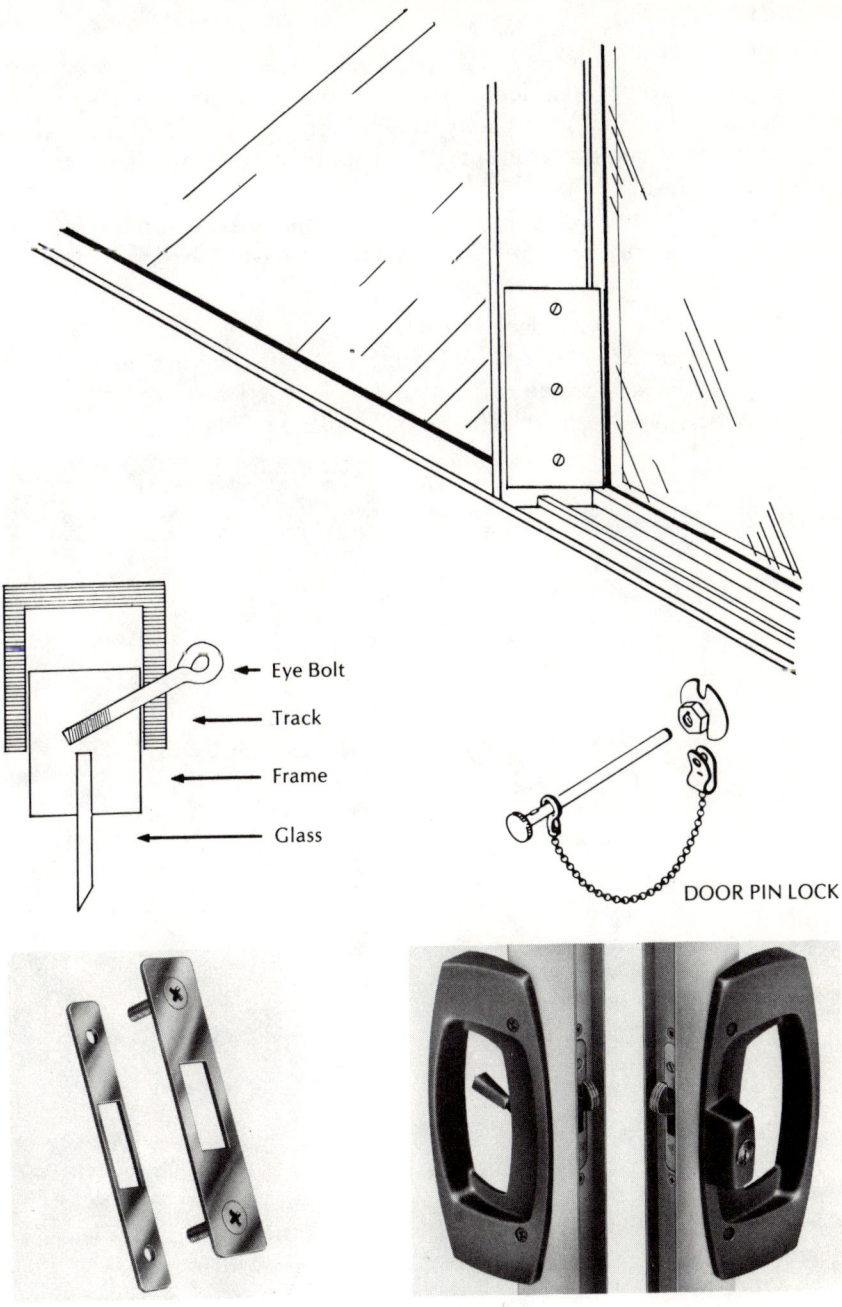

← Eye Bolt
← Track
← Frame
← Glass

DOOR PIN LOCK

STRIKE PLATE
(Model MS 4804)

LOCKSET
(Model MS 5400)

Padlocks and Hasps

When buying padlocks and hasps people get about what they pay for. If you spend two or three dollars you'll get two or three dollars' worth of protection. Considering that padlocks and hasps are used to protect valuable property in garages, workshops, and sheds, it seems foolhardy to use anything but the best.

When protecting valuable property use a lock that can prevent all but the most severe entry measures. Such a lock must have at least the following qualities for maximum protection:

1. A solid brass or hardened-steel body
2. A hardened-steel shackle at least three-eighths-inch in diameter
3. Toe-and-heel locking
4. A lock that doesn't release the key until the padlock is closed

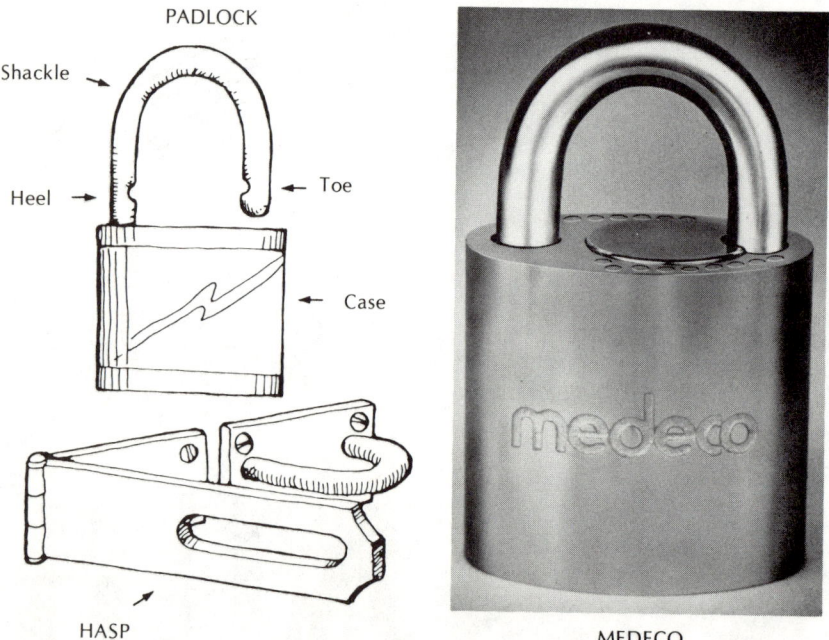

For a top-quality lock that is virtually pick proof try using Medeco or Abloy. For a lock that can be purchased at your local hardware store try the top of the line from Yale, Schlage, Segal, and Master.

A good lock must have an equally strong hasp. If the hasp is weak, a thief just works on the hasp. A crowbar or large screwdriver is often all that is necessary to wrench the hasp from the wall. Use case-hardened steel hasps fastened with bolts that are concealed when the padlock is locked on the hasp.

RESIDENTIAL SECURITY

Good locks are priced as high as $20 and more, so you may want to take further precautions to protect the lock itself. Weld a length of light chain on the shackle that can be bolted to the wall or door next to the side of the hasp that has the U-ring. This will safeguard the lock and ensure that it will always be available when needed. Further, a thief cannot come along and replace your lock with a lock he can open later.

Keyless Locks

A new and innovative protective device is the combination door lock. Some of these locks have a combination head such as those on a safe. Others are like the lock made by Preso-Matic Keyless Locks. The most impressive model has a one-inch deadbolt of case-hardened steel with a combination faceplate that has ten numbered buttons and a reset bar. These faces have accessories that blend with any decor. They are made to install in a door 1¾-inches deep but they have adjustable spacer plates for doors from 1⅜-inch to 2¼-inches deep. The spacers reportedly do not detract from the security of the locks. Preso-Matic Model LT8102 has the one-inch deadbolt and comes in four- and seven-number combinations. On the inside is a day-lock device offering the occupant easy locking while at home. The price for something so effective is quite modest, as compared to other door-locking devices. A seven-digit combination gives the burglar a one-in-ten-million chance to pick your lock.

Each home should have at least one door with an access that does not require use of a key.

PRESO-MATIC "HERCULES" MODEL LT-8102 has a one-inch deadbolt of case-hardened steel. The bolt is made to revolve in place hindering any saw blade activity. The seven-digit combination is preferred, not only because it is harder to pick but because it is much harder for the casual observer to remember the combination and open later. Use in conjunction with a normal door knob. (Courtesy of Preso-Matic Lock Company, Inc.)

Key Control

A great many burglaries occur without the need for any sort of forcible entry. Instead, burglars gain access by obtaining the homeowners' keys—often from a parking attendant or a mechanic or from some other person who has temporary possession of the keys. The burglars simply copy the keys left with them, and—with a little ingenuity—they get an address. Then they wait for the right time.

You can minimize the likelihood of a theft from a burglar using your own keys by following these basic instructions:

1. Never have identification tags on your keys.
2. When you move into a new home or apartment have the locks changed or re-keyed by a locksmith. This is a good time to upgrade your locks.
3. Don't give your keys to acquaintances. They may not be thieves, but they may not be as careful as you are either. If you must give your keys to someone else be sure you only give them the keys to the car or for whatever item it is you are loaning. There are two-part key rings available that can separate your keys easily.
4. Never hide your keys outside. Burglars count on finding keys outside to help with many of their entries.
5. Scratch off any identifying numbers on padlocks and keys after you purchase them to prevent someone from taking down the number and having a new key made.

WINDOWS

There are three main types of windows: sliding, double-hung, and hinged. In every home I have ever visited the builder has installed locking devices good only for keeping out honest people. The locks used in the windows have a simple latch that can be easily reached by a screwdriver.

A burglar is generally very fearful about glass. He does not want to make noise by shattering it and he does not want accidental damage to himself from breaking it. So he will attempt many different means of entry before he will resort to breaking glass. The sound of a loud bang or the busting of wood may go unnoticed but glass-breaking nearly always draws attention.

Your objective, therefore, is to install well-laid-out locking devices on your windows that will cause a burgular to make a lot of noise to gain entry. If the burglar can be stalled for as long as four to six minutes the chance that he will go look for easier victims increases drastically with each passing minute.

Windows should always be kept locked. They should be kept clear of any kind of foliage that might give a hiding place to a burglar while he attempts entry. I believe that keyed locks for windows are dangerous: they tend to keep you in more effectively than they keep thieves out. If a fire or other emergency occurs you may not have time to locate the right keys. You can always break the window, but so can a burglar. There are simple ways to lock your windows without jeopardizing your family's safety.

Double-Hung Windows

A simple method for securing a double-hung window is to drill a hole on an angle through the top frame of the lower window and partially into the lower frame of the upper window. The hole that goes into the upper window's lower frame should not penetrate more than three-quarters of the width of the frame. An eyebolt inserted into the hole prevents the window from being opened. The eyebolt can then be secured to the lower window frame by a screw and a short piece of chain or string. This way the eyebolts are always accessible.

Again, there are steel pin security locks available on the market that can do the same job as the eyebolt.

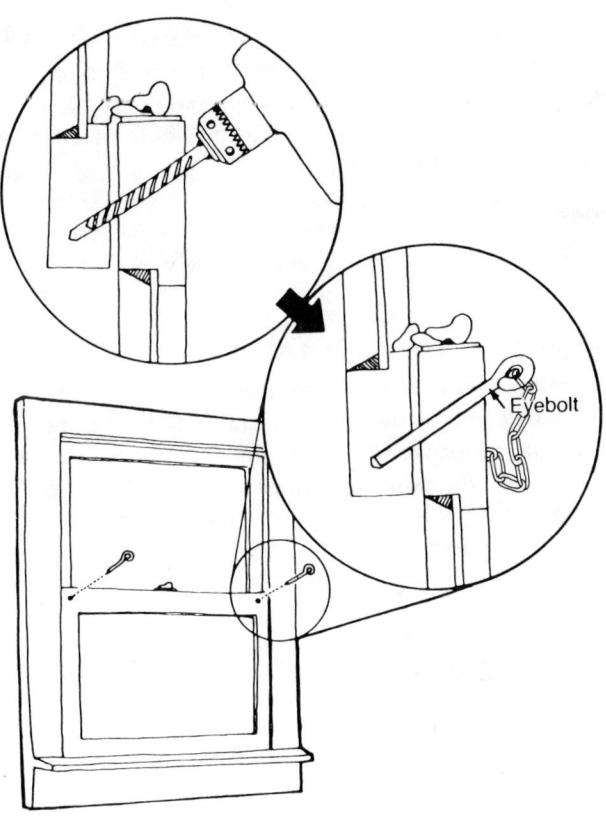

If you like your windows open for fresh air you can drill a hole in the guide-frame just above the lower window in the proper open position.

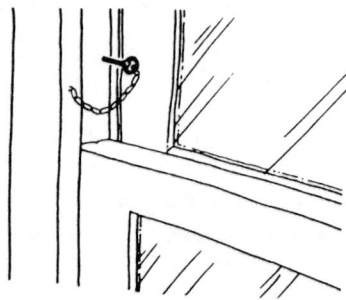

For further protection you can use eyebolts with a wood-screw base. Drill a regular hole into the frame, but do not drill as deep as the length of the bolt. Make the bolt set out half an inch. Use a smaller drill bit and drill the remaining distance. When inserted, the eyebolt will stop short of a complete penetration and will then have to be screwed in which gives a very secure fit.

There are few ways to protect your glass against breakage. One way is to install wrought-iron bars or metal grating to the outside of your windows. This procedure provides security for the homeowner, but you must be sure that at least one window in each room has a release mechanism that will enable you to get out in an emergency.

Sliding Windows

Sliding windows can be secured in the same way that sliding doors are secured.

Hinged Windows

Hinged windows may be a problem if the frames are lightweight metal. Any locking device can be only as strong as the frame it is attached to. Perhaps, if enough metal or wood is available, the best device would be a throw-bolt secured to the outward swinging side of the window. Have the bolt enter the window frame with at least a half-inch purchase. Eyebolts or steel pins may be usable if there is some substance to the window frame.

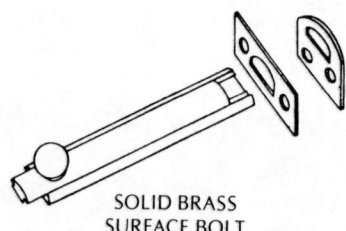

SOLID BRASS
SURFACE BOLT

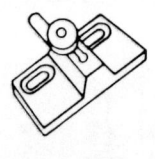

SLIDING DOOR &
WINDOW LOCK

COOPERATIVE CONSTRUCTION

Your goal in making physical changes to your property should be to accomplish these ends:

1. Give no means for a person or persons to hide easily on your property.
2. Create barriers that discourage criminal activities.
3. Provide a safe position in your home where you can readily see your entire grounds.
4. Do not have the appearance of your residence different from others in your neighborhood. You don't want your home singled out as either the most prosperous or the most vulnerable.

Shrubs and Trees

The first physical change necessary is to eliminate places where a potential thief or aggressor can hide on your property.

You should cut any tree branches that are seven feet or less from ground level. Do not cut trees down unless absolutely necessary. Trees shorter than seven feet should be treated as shrubs.

Trim down every shrub so it has no more than three square feet of surface on each side and is a couple of feet away from the next shrub. Never leave a bush that is more than three feet high, and if it is less than three feet high it should be only one foot wide. Go to the street in front of your house and take a look. If someone could hide more than half of himself behind any bush, trim it.

Remove any hedges that border yours and a neighbor's property lines.

Cut ground cover such as ivy or trim it so that no one can hide in it.

Those nice plants that gave you such a feeling of seclusion are now a liability. If you must have the plants you will have to realize that they may well be a source of trouble for you in the future.

Fencing

Fencing for your yard should be in good taste: no barbed wire or razor-wire tops. Your objective should be to eliminate hiding places and make it difficult to get beyond the fence. The leading edge of your house should be your guiding line for fencing. The fence should be at least six feet high. If you have a block wall, it would be best to top the wall with wrought iron. The wrought iron can be decorative, but make sure the top is not constructed with rounded edges; make the top arrowheads or points. If your block wall is five or six feet high, give it an extra two feet of wrought iron.

Most cities require permits to construct a fence over six feet high. Therefore, I would suggest applying for permits before construction begins.

Construct dog runs in out-of-the-way areas, using them to cut your backyard off from an aggressor's approach. Keep your dogs in areas that need the most protection: back wall, side lots, or other out-of-the-way areas.

Roofing

When crime rates go up due to shortages or civil unrest, fire could be a tool of the lawless. If your roofing is due to be replaced why not eliminate another source of potential danger to your family by replacing the roofing material with a non-combustible material such as Spanish tile or any one of a number of other synthetic roofs.

GUARD DOGS

Most humans are afraid of the rage of a dog. When tear gas, guns, clubs, and police fail, trained dogs will always back down a mob. A gun or club may hurt them, and tear gas will distract or infuriate them, but a dog's bite or the threat of one will terrify the mob. (I'm not sure why, but it does, and that's what counts.)

Remember: a dog that barks vigorously at a stranger will never have to bite. Guard dogs that bite strangers also bite their owners, and anyone else for that matter. They are just plain mean. The dog I want to recommend is all bark and no bite.

The object is to train your non-biting dog as a watchdog rather than as an attack dog. There are good books on this subject. I recommend you read them and train your dog not only to be a watchdog, but also obedience-train him. Remember that a large part of training a dog is training yourself. Always use the same terms and commands. Be very consistent.

If you train your dog the way I train mine it is very simple. The first step is to get several people not known to your dog to act as aggressors. Put your dog in your yard behind the fence. Always use your own yard and have the "stranger" enter by the front entrance. Stay with your dog to reinforce his behavior. If the dog barks when the stranger enters, praise him. Once you praise him, the dog will probably stop barking. So have the stranger jump toward the dog, making mean noises, as soon as the dog stops barking. While the dog is still barking, have the stranger run out of the yard—fast. If the dog stops barking before the stranger gets out of the yard, the stranger should immediately become aggressive until the dog barks again.

The idea is for the dog to bark the entire time a stranger is in the yard, but only when the stranger is in the yard. Repeat this process until the dog learns that when a stranger is present he barks. The stranger is responsible for making the dog bark—he must tease, jump at, or yell at the dog to make him aggressive. As soon as the dog is riled up, the stranger must leave quickly.

Usually a training session will need no more than fifteen to twenty minutes a day. Once the dog barks when the stranger enters the yard, the training should end until the next day. Owner and aggressor should have nothing to do with each other at this point.

This training should become consistent, whether it takes two or three days, or even two months. Once this training seems to be effective, other strangers must enter the yard with the same effect. The dog must bark at all people as they enter the yard. "Friends" should come in and, if the dog's bark is fierce, the owner should verbally soothe the dog. The dog, after some practice should be able to tell from the tone of your voice whether or not a person is a possible threat. The only way he'll know is to have you show him. After the strangers leave your yard you must praise your dog—every time—and thank him for scaring those nasty people away.

The second step—and just as important as the first—is to teach your dog *not* to attack. You may not think this is important, but it is, mainly for your own and your friends' and neighbors' protection. It is best to educate your dog to prevent him from ever aggressively hurting someone since you never want to have that problem to contend with.

The best way I have found is to bring the stranger back, but first put a long, strong check-cord on the dog. Hold the cord at the end, tightly. Let the stranger stand just out of reach of the dog with the dog's check-cord fully extended. Have the stranger tease the dog into an aggressive attack. When the dog lunges or jumps at the stranger, hold tight on the cord and pull back, scolding the dog loudly. If the dog lunges so fast that he uses the full extension of the cord, his feet will come out from under him. This—combined with scolding—should reinforce the idea that active assaults are forbidden.

Let the stranger walk through the back yard, and as long as the dog is barking the stranger should ignore the dog. When the dog stops barking, the stranger should become aggressive until barking continues. While this is going on you should have a firm grip on the cord and never let the dog go unscolded for lunging at the stranger. Remember, unless you want your dog to act aggressively toward your friends, do not treat the stranger with anything but aggressive, loud talk. Be angry at the stranger; do not be friendly in any way. The dog should get the idea after a few times, perhaps after a few weeks of drill.

Even with strangers you are going to want your dog to stop barking and to heel at your command. Practice command training now. Use at least two commands and train the dog well. Use the command "Down!" to stop the dog from barking. Take his muzzle firmly in your hand and close his mouth to stop the barking. Then reassure and praise him.

Give him only verbal praise, pats, and petting. Never use food rewards for a working dog. You will want to use the command "Heel!" to keep the dog at your side. Just pull him to your left side and praise him. A lot of repetition is necessary for complete obedience. Use your check-cord. Stand away from him. Say, "Heel!" and pull the dog to your left side. As soon as he is sitting at your left, no matter how hard it was to get him there, praise him.

The commands "Down" or "Heel" do not have to be used with your dog. Just pick a word and stick with it. Remember—train the master, then train the dog.

ALARM SYSTEMS

The basics of alarm systems are really quite simple. They just seem to be complex on first glance. The mass of switches and wire contacts really work down to a very simple system. The alarm system must have a control panel hooked up to the power supply, inputs, and alarm signals.

The control panel receives and evaluates inputs, activates alarm signals, has 110-volt plug-in, battery backup with automatic charge, and terminal box. Some control panels have time delay, automatic reset, and annunciators that give the location of an alarm. Area sensors can be ultrasonic, microwave, photoelectric, audio or sound, or seismic. Contact sensors can be magnetic contact switches, vibration or shock sensors, pressure-sensitive sensors, foil, or panic switches. Alarm signals are bells, horns, or sirens which are activated at a central station, at a police alarm board, or at the owner's residence or place of business.

Control Panels

Control panels are extremely varied in cost and use. They range from $25 for an automobile panel to several thousand dollars for a computer system with graphic display panels. The simplest system converts a power source into a usable range that sends a current through a line. When the current is broken, a switch triggers an alarm. The most extravagant systems have video display terminals, central processors, graphic display panels, and print-out devices. These systems are generally used on premises that have many means of access which require a large number of sensors. Most homeowners do not require such elaborate systems.

The control unit on a home system should have at least the following features:

1. Automatic reset capability. (Some states require that an alarm reset itself after six minutes in case of a false alarm.)
2. Ability to accept all types of sensors—normally open and normally closed. (Normally open has a current going through it at all times.)
3. Auxiliary power (generally a 12-volt battery pack with recharger).
4. Twenty-four-hour audible panic circuit (to sound alarm when danger threatens you while you are home alone).
5. Supervised keyswitch to turn alarms on and off.

6. At least a two-zone capability (which will enable residents to activate exterior alarms and deactivate interior sensors such as ultrasonic or microwave systems when they are home).

To enhance a basic system you could also have these capabilities:
1. Zones shown on a control panel to show where an intruder has entered.
2. Automatic telephone dialer (to call the police or fire departments as needed).
3. Heat and smoke detectors for fire protection.
4. Entry delay (in conjunction with keyed entry switch).
5. Panic switches placed throughout the house.

Input Sensors

Input sensors can be installed using wire or small battery-operated transmitters. Wire installations placed in the walls and attic may well add value to the home and are far more reliable than transmitters although they cost more. The homeowner or renter may have transmitters installed to avoid the more costly wire installation.

An input sensor is a device that activates an alarm system to create an alarm. These devices have many forms, but usually they either close an open circuit or open a closed circuit to cause an alarm. Think of them in terms of a wall switch: turn on the switch and a light goes on; with an input sensor an alarm goes on. The area sensors are capable of noting a change in the environment. This trips a switch which causes an alarm.

Magnetic contact switches consist of two parts: a magnet, and a self-contained magnetically operated switch. The magnet is mounted on a door or window and the switching device is mounted on the door frame or window frame. A magnetic field is generated when a door or window is closed and the two parts are brought into proximity. When the door or window is opened the magnetic field is interrupted and an alarm sounds. These switches are either normally open or normally closed. A normally open switch, when activated, closes the circuit, causing an alarm. With the normally closed switch, the current flows through the switch continually until the current is stopped (such as by the door opening) which causes an alarm.

Foil is a thin metallic tape that is used to protect windows. The tape is a normally closed system with current flowing through the tape until the window or tape is broken which causes an alarm. Since the tape is apt to be unsightly it is seldom used in residences. Further, it tends to break easily which can cause many malfunctions and generate costly repairs. Window protection is best accomplished through the use of vibration or shock sensors.

Vibration or shock sensors are contact microphones that detect sound vibrations in the body of the protected material. The signals are fed into an amplifier unit where the sensitivity control determines the sound level necessary to sound the alarm. These sensors should have a short time delay to prevent false alarms from a single impulse.

Pressure-sensitive sensors are weight-sensitive switches or mats that are placed in entrances or hallways to announce, through the alarm system, a person's presence. The mats can be sensitive to water and should be purchased with this in mind. Manufacturers of these sensors carry a line of mats that can withstand water exposure, but you must specifically request these. The mats can be purchased with pressure sensitivity ranging from five to twenty pounds.

Area Sensors

Ultrasonic sensors receive inaudible soundwaves that are emitted from the sensor. When an intruder enters, the wave pattern is altered which changes the frequency and activates the alarm. Ultrasonic devices are not affected by heavy rains or condensation. Further, they can detect a person's presence even if the person is hidden in the building. They are also self-restoring which means they will activate upon the movement of an intruder, re-balance when the movement stops and sound another alarm when further movement is detected.

Some disadvantages of area sensors:

1. Sounds, such as bells and telephones, might set off false alarms.
2. If the contents of the room are moved or changed in the building, dead areas might develop to hamper the system.
3. Drafts caused by open or broken windows may cause false alarms.
4. A very slow-moving intruder might go undetected.
5. Soft goods, such as acoustic ceilings and cardboard, could reduce the system's effectiveness because ultrasonic sound waves do not penetrate these soft goods but are absorbed by them.

All in all, the device can be used effectively in a home environment provided the above shortcomings are recognized and proper precautions are taken.

Microwave sensors are electromagnetic fields which are activated in the presence of motion in the area of protection. These devices are not sensitive to sound or air turbulence. The unit consists of a transmitter and a receiver. Radio frequency transmitter signals are beamed from the transmitter into the secured area, striking stationary objects and reflecting back to the receiver. The receivers disregard signals presented by stationary objects. However, when something moves through the field of protection the signals received by the receiver are reflected back at a different rate which causes the device to trigger an alarm. The microwave motion detector can be transmitted in a rather precise directional pattern. This feature makes it possible for the alarm installer to cover a wide range of areas of different sizes. The devices can be made to cover narrow hallways to 300 feet in length or to saturate areas up to 10,000 square feet.

It is important to note that microwaves can pass through windows, light doors, and walls of various substances or can be reflected by metallic substances. (This can and does cause false alarms if the system is not properly installed. Consequently, the installation of this system can be very difficult.)

Because microwaves pass through some walls and doors they have the added advantage of being capable of providing coverage for more than one room. A microwave transmitter may be placed in a living room facing into the house and actually be capable of noting a presence in two adjoining rooms.

A few basic principles must be observed while installing this device:

1. Never face the transmitter toward doors or windows where people casually walking by may trigger an alarm.

2. Care must be taken not to direct a microwave unit toward any metalic surfaces which might cause a bouncing effect and set off an alarm.

3. Discriminator circuits are installed into the system to eliminate false alarms. As a result, normal motion of machines such as small motor-driven fans will not cause false alarms, but if many such devices are on, they might cause a cumulative effect and overload the discriminator which may cause a false alarm.

A microwave system facing into a house and avoiding external exposure can provide a very good source of area protection if installation is done properly.

Photoelectric devices are invisible switching devices. An invisible infrared light beam is transmitted from a transmitter to a receiver. When any object moves in front of the light and breaks the beam the alarm is sounded. These devices must be perfectly aligned. If the transmitter or receiver is struck it could change the direction of the beam and the system would fail to function. Bright lights, such as car lights, paralyze the system so that alarms fail to sound.

Audio systems consists of a sensitive microphone, or microphones, that transmit sound to the alarm system. These systems have been designed to screen out extraneous sounds normally found within the dwelling. The most reliable system has a discriminator device that accumulates sound to the point of overload when the alarm sounds.

ALARM SIGNALS

There are four different ways to announce an intruder's presence: local alarm; central station alarm; proprietary alarm; police department alarm. Under normal circumstances your alarm system should announce itself to the most professional receiver, such as the police department. (Problems with alarm signals do arise and will be covered in the list that follows.)

Police Department Alarm

The police departments in many cities are now accepting direct connection of alarms into their central station. Upon activation of the alarm on the owner's premises, the police receive an instantaneous call announcing an intruder's presence on those premises.

Automatic dialers can be installed in a home or business that will automatically dial the police and announce, with a prerecorded message, that a burglary is in progress and give necessary information such as address and names of the occupants. There are also direct-line hookups, through telephone lines, that give owners a system continually monitored by police.

Problems occur when police departments experience excessive numbers of false alarms. These tend to negate the effectiveness of these alarm systems because response-times fall off. Some cities are passing ordinances which specify that after a pre-determined number of false alarms have been received the police department may take the system off and not respond at all.

Unfortunately the problem goes even further than problems with false alarms. Police departments are now approaching their level of saturation. They no longer, in most cases, have enough manpower to cope with the problems of protecting property. With an ever-increasing workload the capability of response of police departments is on a decline that could have very serious consequences for the general public.

A further problem arises in cases where the police do respond to an alarm only to find no signs of forcible entry. After a few minutes the police report a false alarm because they cannot get into the house without a key and there is no sign to indicate that a burglar is inside. But, in some cases, a burglar has entered through an open window and he gets away with the crime in spite of the alarm's connection to the police.

Central Station Alarm

The central station system does not usually have a local alarm bell or horn. Following an illegal entry, a silent alarm is broadcast to the central station of a private alarm company. From there a call is made to the local police. The private company will then dispatch a patrolman to assist the police in assessing the building and resetting the alarm. In order to be cost-effective an alarm company must have several hundred alarm inputs at its central station. A single alarm sounding presents no problem, but if more alarms sound than there are patrolmen, then unfortunately the alarm company may face some of the same problems the police departments face.

As times become harder and thefts increase, alarm companies and private security must be capable of taking up the slack where the police leave off.

Proprietary Alarm

Proprietary alarms take two forms. In the first type, the owner of a business may have a central guard station on the premises where all alarm systems are monitored. Large facilities use this system quite well where a secured command post is used to monitor the system while other guards are on patrol and capable of answering a radio dispatch. An off-premises central station should also be used in case of a hostage situation or jeopardy to the guards themselves.

The second system, in which the owner of the system is to be notified in an emergency, is not quite so effective. The owner of the business or residence will have a second location on line where he spends most of his time. An alarm at the business would be reported to him at home. Further, if it is his home that is broken into, the dialer (or direct-line system) would announce this problem to him at his business. The obvious problem is what happens during an absence from both places? The cost of such an elaborate system almost demands that the system be monitored by professionals.

Local Alarms

I believe that a local alarm which sounds on the premises is the most valuable of any alarm system. Most often the reason for installing an alarm is to protect the premises from thefts, not to apprehend thieves. It would be nice to help the police apprehend thieves but that is secondary to the issue, which is to stop the thief from stealing your property. If the thief is capable of entering your property, and even if he is aware that a silent alarm has gone off, he will still know that it will take the police many minutes to respond. He has time for a quick grab.

Perhaps a burglar has arranged for several alarms to be set across town from where he is and he knows that the trip from across town will take the police ten minutes—all he needs for his job. But if he is confronted with a loud, shrill siren, inside and out when he enters the premises, and maybe with very bright strobe lights as well, what do you think he is going to do? Even the most professional burglar will be unnerved by this: he knows the police have probably been notified; he has an extreme dose of adrenaline; he recognizes the possibility that a zealous neighbor will come charging in ready to shoot at the first shadow; and, unless he takes time to try to disarm the alarm, he can no longer hear approaching trouble.

All in all, the thief has got to believe that this job is over and that there may be easier pickings down the street. He will probably get out knowing that his chances of pulling off the job have now decreased and his likelihood of being discovered have increased beyond a reasonable point.

Local alarms are usually bells and sirens placed in some obscure position out of reach, such as under an eave. (The alarms are on the outside to wake up neighbors or to announce the trouble to a passer-by.) I think that a further system installed in the building that shrieks an alarm close to the culprit will do him more damage than would a neighbor charging in with a shotgun. Obvious arrangements must be made.

Alarms placed inside the premises must be capable of being turned off independently of the outside alarm horn so the system can be armed when the homeowner is at home with the alarm system turned on. Also installed should be a lighting system that will have the same effect as the alarm. The lights that seem to be most effective are strobe lights although any flashing lights will help.

CHOOSING AN ALARM

Many of you will decide that an alarm company's installation is desirable. If you decide this make sure your alarm system has several minimum characteristics.

When at home:

Always have most of your system capable of being turned on while you are up and around in your home. This part of the system is door and window switches. When you're in the house these switches will still be capable of ringing your primary alarm.

Have a portion of your system in devices that detect outside presences. Do not have this system do anything more than ring a buzzer or turn on a light. It should announce to you when you are home that someone is in your yard or possibly around your cars. Every time a human walks on your property, you'll be aware of it. There will come a day when this will be an extremely valuable aid.

When away:

The system to use when you are not at home should include perimeter switches and possibly microwave or ultrasonic sensors. These devices should be used in conjunction with an automatic telephone dialer that has line-siezure capability and should also call at least one back-up number. Your system should also ring a local alarm, sound an inside siren, and activate strobe lights while you are away.

There are so many alarm components on the market today that there is no one place a person can go to obtain a recommendation on any particular system. Underwriters' Laboratories (UL) has certified that certain alarm systems are what they claim to be, but UL has rated only a very small percentage of available systems and does not give price information. The following is an example of alarm systems which can be installed by following instruction sheets included with the purchase.

ALARM: You may purchase an alarm for thousands of dollars or you may buy a do-it-yourself kit. If you buy a system like this one you would probably want an inside and outside bell or siren as well as strobe lights inside. (Courtesy of Aqualarm Inc.)

CHOOSING AN ALARM COMPANY

Individuals or businesses that decide to purchase an alarm system may go through a very risky process of checking out competitive bids from different companies which often results in the purchase of the cheapest—but not necessarily the most reliable—system.

Components, such as magnetic switches, can range from 75 cents to four dollars in dealer's cost. Microwave and ultrasonic systems, as well as all the other components, have a wide range of prices and abilities. The low bidder could be purchasing low-quality merchandise with a very short life span while a higher bidder could use top-of-the-line products.

There are approximately one million alarm systems available to the public in this country. Some manufacturers deal in the most reliable product, others in the cheapest. Some have all products available and will sell you whatever you want.

The following are some basic suggestions that may help guide you in your selection of an alarm company and its products:

1. Underwriters' Laboratories has certified 75,000 different alarm systems. Get bids on UL-approved systems.

2. Find someone who has had an alarm in service for some time and ask for a recommendation for an alarm company in your area.

3. Have the alarm company itemize its bid, indicating manufacturers and model numbers of the components so that other alarm companies can bid on the same items.

There are more economical ways of providing protection when harder times arrive. A person will have to use his imagination to improvise further security measures. Surely everyone has seen the string-pulling device that turns on a light hung from the ceiling. This type of switch can have many uses in a security system. What would happen if a person trying to climb your wall should reach up and grab a string on the top of your wall and all of a sudden a bright light shown down on him? If he had any thoughts of climbing over, he surely would forget them. This light switch could also activate a bell in your house by simply using the electrical leads from the light itself to send a current through a normally dormant line.

Your yard could also have trip lines, of similar design, if there are no animals that could trip the device. Most commercial alarms are nothing but switches, normally open or normally closed. You can buy switches and install them yourself. An alarm company makes money because the job they do looks professional. The basics are simple. There is just a lot of work in installing. The problem lies in selecting the right type of device to suit your needs. If you are only interested in perimeter security a simple switch system can be installed with little money but a lot of work. Use magnetic contact switches and pressure sensitive sensors to encircle your home.

CONSTRUCTING HIDING PLACES

I have tried to make as many economical suggestions as possible for bringing security within the reach of people without large budgets. Security devices are expensive. As a result, people tend to put off purchasing them. In this section I will help you design hiding places that will enhance your chances of keeping thieves from your valuables even if they get in your home or business and have time to ransack it.

First, consider your home for a minute. Walk through it, but don't just look—see it. Look at the mass of cabinets and closets. See the many pictures, the furniture, wood adornments, plastic parts and fixtures. It's an intricate maze, one of confusion and random patterns.

If it's such a confused maze, what makes it so easy for the thief to steal your valuables? Thieves know where people usually put their valuables: the china cabinet for the silver and crystal; the dresser and closet for jewelry and money; the den or bedrooms for guns. A thief knows almost instinctively where to go and what to expect in any house. But you can create an environment where a thief won't find things in their customary places—in fact won't find them at all. Some hiding places are easy to make and are easily overlooked by any thief. A thief can't afford the time to search your house for hours to find your valuables. It's simpler for him to just assume that you don't have valuables in your home.

Baseboard Vault

In deciding to construct hiding places you should make an inventory of the amount and kind of valuables you need to hide. If you require only a few square inches of very secure space, the wall baseboard may offer a solution. The baseboard is simply pried from the wall, your valuables are hidden, and the baseboard is refinished to match the baseboard around it to protect its secrecy. Don't consider the project unless you intend to create a perfectly concealed hiding place.

The right baseboard must be small enough to be managed easily. Look through your home in the corners and in the closets. Find a suitable small section of board that won't be kicked or tampered with accidentally.

Once you have found the right board you must be very careful. If your baseboard paint has formed a seal with the wall gently use a knife to separate the baseboard from the wall. If the baseboard separates well, and the cut does not seem obvious, you may be able to avoid painting or expensive repairs. Baseboards are usually attached by several headless nails. These nails can be removed. The trick is to remove them without damaging the baseboard's appearance. You may be able to remove the board by putting a not-too-sharp tool under the board and prying directly outward just below the nails. This should be done slowly and gradually so that pry-marks or breaks don't occur.

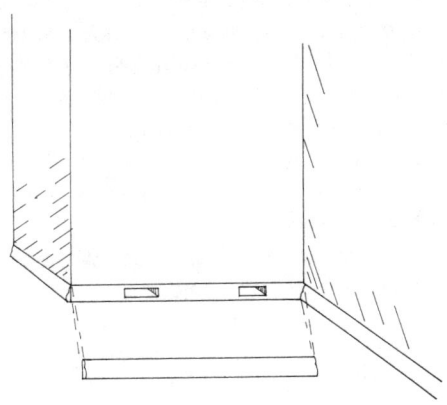

BASEBOARD VAULT

After you have removed the board your work has just begun. You could be one of the lucky ones who open up the baseboard and find a hiding place already there. But nearly always you will find a 2-by-4 supporting the wall studs. You will have to drill and chisel a cavity out of the 2-by-4 for your valuables. You may or may not have to go through plaster to reach the 2-by-4. Be very careful that work you do does not appear above the line of the baseboard. Once you have hollowed out the space you need, your job is all but done. You only have to fasten the baseboard back in place. You could use many devices to accomplish this task. Velcro could be glued to the baseboard and to the wall. Make sure the Velcro is fastened in a way that doesn't make the baseboard protrude, possibly by recessing the Velcro into the wall to create a close fit. Magnetic cabinet latches can be used about every six inches. These should also be recessed into the wall. Other cabinet-latching devices could be used as well. Remember that the outward appearance is most important. You must not leave any evidence that the baseboard has been tampered with.

Cedar Chest in the Floor

Some valuables are quite large. Many people value their guns, antiques, and silverware more than they value their money and jewelry.

In a home with hardwood floors a compartment can be made to conceal large valuables under the floor. (People who have concrete slabs or who live in apartments will have to use other means to hide their valuables.) The simplicity of this project can be deceiving. Be sure you are committed to completing the project before you start.

After you read the following instructions completely and determine the size you want, you should construct a box large enough to handle the items you want to be hidden but not too large to fit in the area under your floor.

If you want to hide guns make the box a rectangle which is long enough to hold guns lying down. The box should be made out of solidly constructed material, at least ¾-inch thick. Seal it with a good putty and paint it inside and out to make it as moisture-proof as possible. Make a partial lid on top of the box. The lid should have an opening approximately two feet square or large enough so that you can get all your valuables inside. Keep in mind that once the box is partially filled it might be more difficult to put long or large items in the door of the chest.

To find a place for your hiding place below the floor keep floor location and below-the-floor location in mind. An area with carpeting is usually best to hide this device. If you don't have carpeting you can use a throw rug when you've finished the project. A carpeted closet is convenient—it gets little traffic and you can always conceal your hiding place further with shoes. Another good place is under the bed. I doubt whether many beds have been moved by burglars in their search for booty.

Before you cut the carpet or wood on your floor check that the coast is clear under the floor. Crawl into the area under the house and, with the help of a person stationed on the floor above, determine where the spot is and, if there are no obstructions, begin by drilling four small holes up through the floor at the corners of your intended hole. (Never cut main floor beams. Cut between them so that your box can use them for support.) Your floor hole must be several inches larger than the box that goes into the hole. If you want more room than is available between beams you may have to cut two channels out of the box for the beams to fit into.

After the first four holes have been drilled and something inserted into them so that you can find them from above, you can continue to cut the hole from above. Be especially careful not to damage the carpet—you may not be able to match it later. Use a knife and a yardstick to cut the carpet from hole to hole, being careful not to damage the nap any more than necessary. Cut your pad out carefully as well; you'll need that to maintain the proper level.

After you have cut out your floor boards, you can install the box. If you have made the box the same width as the beams your job will be a lot easier. Simply raise your box up from underneath and, while it is held in place, drill holes through the beam into the box and attach nuts and bolts. Use round-head bolts under the house that will be tightened down from within the box itself. Be sure that the hole in the box matches the hole in your floor. The box-hole should overlap about two inches all the way around the floor hole. This will provide a lip for your door.

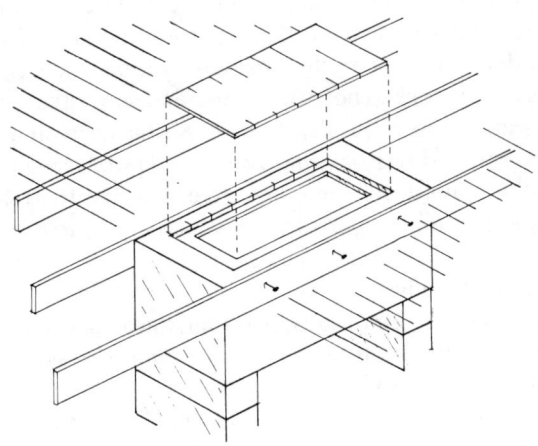

CEDAR CHEST IN THE FLOOR

While you are working under the house you should do several things. First, place bricks or other material under your box to support the weight it will contain. Second, and most important, seal off all remaining cracks and paint the area well. After you have painted you might tape potential cracks with duct tape for a little more security. Moisture under a house can be very damaging to your valuables if you don't take every possible precaution.

Some hardwood floors have plywood layered under the hardwood. When you are determining the depth of the door keep this in mind. Measure your opening and cut a piece of plywood, or other wood, to take the place of removed sections of floor board. After you have a door of exact size that fits tightly, paint the wood with moisture-resistant paint. Glue the carpet padding to the wood and then glue the carpet to the padding. You can use a bent screwdriver to reach into the holes you drilled earlier to lift the door out. You may also use a security cam lock that mounts flush to the floor.

Look for other hiding places where there are dead spaces: between beams in the walls; under that loose brick; in the ceiling beyond the ceiling tile; under the stairs. There are many ways to do it: find your own and make sure no one except your spouse knows its location.

NEIGHBORHOOD SECURITY
Steering Committee

In a neighborhood environment a primary issue should be neighborhood cooperation. Talk to your neighbors as a group or individually. Most likely they will recognize the need for cooperative help as you do. The first step is to establish a cooperative neighborhood security procedure.

After you have searched out people who are interested in protecting their homes collectively, you should meet and elect a steering committee. This committee should consist of at least seven members from individual households so that each committee member can be in charge of activities on one day of each week. The committee, and any other interested residents, should outline objectives and goals. A chairman should be elected after a number of meetings have taken place. He or she should have the agreement of the majority of the committee. You are there to provide for the common good of your neighborhood—in this case, to protect your lives and property.

Remember that police and civil authorities are particularly afraid of "vigilante" type activity, and rightly so. Vigilantes take the law into their own hands, causing further problems for the police. Consider inviting someone from the police department to attend your committee meetings.

In the early stages do not talk about guns, uniforms, or guards. You should be well started before things get that bad. If your plans entail fencing off streets, remember that your city government has to give permission. Take care of this early, before the need actually arises.

At first, it will be time for homes to change in appearance so they will be more visible, and for the neighborhood to be educated. Do this with the city government's help. If the time comes for stricter security, and if you have performed well, they may take the ball from you and start other groups with like goals. They certainly will be more likely to grant more severe measures.

The following is a reasonable agenda for your first few meetings:
1. Steering committee
2. Police
3. Neighborhood passive watch
4. Alarm procedures
5. Cooperative construction
6. Alarms
7. Timing
8. Dogs for security
9. Education of others
10. Surrounding neighborhoods

Remember, the active involvement of your neighbors creates an environment of self-help and cooperation which may lead to other benefits. Certain neighbors may have skills that could benefit the rest of your neighborhood.

Neighborhood Passive Watch

The basic necessity in your neighborhood security program is a passive watch. This requires that everyone in the neighborhood know their neighbors well: know their automobiles and when they are to be home; be aware of one another's schedules; know the people on each side of you, those across the street, and neighbors behind you so that if someone sees a new face in the yard he can take some sort of action.

The action taken is very important. If the police department is called every time a stranger is seen in your neighborhood, the department could become inundated with—and annoyed by—false alarms. The best first step is to call the neighbor about the stranger in his yard. Possibly the neighbor will say he is a friend. If so, no further action is necessary. If the neighbor doesn't know the stranger, both of you can then take action such as locking doors and windows and watching the stranger's activity. If he appears to be a threat, or if the stranger is still lurking on the property, your neighbor probably will need police protection. But while calling the police, and during daylight hours, a brief blast on his alarm horn (see *Alarm Procedures* below), followed by responses from other neighbors, should discourage any further loitering. During evening hours the security light system (see *Alarm Procedures*) should be turned on as a first warning system, followed by alarm horns for a more severe threat.

Alarm Procedures

There should be some means available to notify your neighbors if problems arise in the neighborhood and to scare off potential aggressors. All neighbors should be provided with alarm horns. If an aggressor hears his victim's alarm go off, and then repeated soundings throughout the neighborhood, the aggressor is likely to feel he has bitten off more than he can chew.

Two alarms are necessary, one to hear and one to see. Equip each home with a loud air horn. Install at least two floodlights on each roof directed away from the house. Operate two sets of floodlights, one in the front yard and one in the back yard.

When an alarm is sounded, each resident will go to the leading edge of their home where the entire front yard can be observed to turn on the floodlights and to repeat the signal heard. A typical code system could be:

1. One short blast: unknown suspicious persons in the neighborhood, front yards, or streets.

2. Two short blasts: unknown suspicious persons in the backyards.

3. Three short blasts: active or most probable danger in the area; a gang in the neighborhood.

4. Two long blasts: someone breaking into a residence, either yours or someone else's (do not repeat more than twice).

5. A ten-second single blast: "all clear" (do not repeat). This should be sounded only by the patrol or committee member after investigation and a determination that everything is okay.

A great deal of this is psychological warfare. If it is followed, you will prevail.

TIMING

Now is the time to act! Install better locks and timers. Install additional fencing. Have a good perimeter alarm system installed. Next Saturday is the day you should start trimming those hedges and trees. Tomorrow evening is a good time for you to talk to your neighbors to see what their feelings are about your crime problems. If your neighbors are at all receptive, now is the time to start a semi-social meeting leading to the forming of a steering committee.

Today, as you read this book, you should make plans to cover these basic steps, in this approximate order:

1. Install proper outside doors.
2. Install proper locks on doors and windows.
3. Put timers on your inside lights and radio.
4. Purchase proper padlocks and hasps.
5. Trim all shrubs and trees.

6. Contact your neighbors and enact a passive watch.
7. Contact your police and invite a representative to your meetings.
8. Start training your watchdog. Even a common burglar will avoid your noisy dog.
9. Install your alarm horn to notify neighbors of trouble.
10. Install or have installed a basic alarm system.
11. Upgrade or build walls or fences on your property.
12. Install outside lights to be left on through the night: two or three in both your front and back yards close to your outer borders.
13. Install security alarm floodlights.
14. Construct a hiding place for your valuables.

Chapter Three

PERSONAL PROTECTION

One of the most difficult things you can concern yourself with is the need for and the use of personal protection. I have had to deal with this problem for many years. People whom I have caused to be arrested have used many forms of aggression on me. They have brandished guns and knives as well as taking an occasional poke at my nose. Looking back on all these incidents, I have noticed several patterns. Whenever any form of aggression has occurred, it has nearly always been for one of the following reasons:

1. I brought myself down to their level of aggression. In other words, upon seeing anger, I retaliated in kind instead of keeping outwardly aloof and calm.

2. I gave my attacker reason to believe he was more capable than I. People tend to underestimate their own abilities and to overestimate the abilities of an unknown foe.

3. I put myself in a compromising position, such as going into a secluded room when I knew a couple of people would be there who really wanted a chance to get me alone with the desire to do me bodily harm.

I realize now that by not acting correctly I created an environment where I could have been seriously hurt.

Most violence occurs between people who are related or who have had some direct prior contact. This should be an indication of a very important fact: most of those who know you have already underestimated you and will be the ones who create a hostile environment. The fact that 75 percent of all murders are perpetrated in acts of rage or passion certainly attests to the fact that things can get out of hand if you let them. When dealing with people, you must recognize that *self-control* is the most important tool you can hold in your arsenal.

In the days to come, crimes of passion or anger and crimes involving theft will be increasing to the point of being uncountable. At the same time police departments will be understaffed and people will find it harder and harder to become involved in someone else's problems. People will see a mugging in progress and say, "Thank God it's not me!" instead of stepping in to do something about it. The importance of people dealing with their own security in a constructive way will also become very important as times get harder.

CRIME AVOIDANCE

One way to deal with crime avoidance is to always stay home and never go out or talk to anyone, keeping all doors and windows closed and locked. Of course this is neither practical nor desirable so we must first create an environment where problems are less likely to occur. In order to do this, let me paint a picture of one of the most likely victims:

Jane Rothchild is a very pretty young girl, five feet tall, twenty-one years old, blonde hair, blue eyes, with a beautiful smile. She is always pleasant and cheerful. She lives with her wealthy parents who just adore her. They show their adoration in many ways, but it stands out best when you look at the two-carat diamond friendship ring or the brand-new red convertible sports car.

About eight-thirty one night, Jane became restless so she decided to get dressed and go down to the plaza to shop. She dressed in short shorts and a sweater.

She walked out to her car parked at the end of a long driveway and got in. While the car was warming up, she took her mirror and straightened her makeup. When she pulled out the car, she decided she would take the back route to town because she liked seeing the moon and stars as she drove down the dark back streets.

When she reached the plaza, she parked her car at the end of the parking area because she didn't want any more nicks in her car's paint from parking too closely to others. It was a balmy summer night so she strolled casually, swinging her purse, toward the nearest plaza entrance. She saw several people leaving and, being in a good mood, casually smiled as she walked past. She spent an hour strolling through the plaza just being a very pleasant person—happy, content, and in love with life.

After the stores closed, she left and walked to her car, got in, and pulled away. Jane was still restless, so she decided she would take a drive in the hills. She drove for about twenty minutes. When she came to a place where young people park, she stopped to admire the scenery.

After luxuriating in the evening breeze and looking down on the city lights, she started her car and left. Jane drove directly home and parked at the end of the driveway, feeling very good about her little excursion. She went into her house and retired for the evening.

In our society today, Jane's evening could have a reasonable chance of success. She could have done all those things without problems. But if things in our society get any worse—which they have and will—Jane's life and property could be in extreme jeopardy. Before looking at Jane's evening again, I want to bring out several important facts.

First, if someone wants enough for something to happen, they will look for ways to make it happen. They may read between the lines to believe it is happening. In Jane's case, her pretty smile and dress could be interpreted by someone as an invitation although she didn't want it to mean that. One person may be looking for pleasant surroundings and see Jane's smile as pleasant surroundings. Another person may be looking for a date, so Jane's smile and clothes are an invitation to make advances toward her. There are still others who, upon seeing Jane, might say, "She's just asking to be attacked or robbed." The fact that Jane dressed to fit her mood of gay abandon doesn't count. She dressed and acted the way she felt, not paying any attention to the reality of her surroundings.

Second, Jane (as do most people) believed that nothing could ever happen to her. Victims are always other people. Or, "That's too scary to think about. If I don't think about it, it won't happen." Or, "Bad things only happen to bad people; they wouldn't dare invade my Shangri-La."

Jane Rothchild's evening wasn't quite so uneventful. As a matter of fact, Jane really had a miserable night. It went something like this:

After she walked down the driveway she found that her expensive convertible had been stolen.

Or, when she got into the car and set her purse down, a kid picked it up and ran.

Or, as she drove through those quiet, secluded streets, a carload of young men saw her, forced her off the road and robbed and raped her. No one was around to protest.

Or, when she parked her car in that secluded parking spot, a man came up to her, pointed a knife at her, and robbed and raped her.

Or, as she strolled toward the plaza and smiled at those people, they believed it was an invitation and became very indignant when Jane objected, so they took what they wanted.

Or, when Jane strolled out of the exit after closing time, two guys that Jane had smiled at earlier followed her.

Or, as Jane reached the area where her car was parked, she found that it had been stolen.

Jane's problems are not uncommon. Today many women have had to undergo the same victimization. Jane didn't recognize her jeopardy. She was naive. Her problems were many and they happened because of a few things she did wrong.

Women should take the following precautions:

1. Dress in the way you expect to be treated. Clothing can communicate many things to observers.

2. Park your vehicles as close to your house as possible. If they are not in a garage, they must be close and clearly visible from the house.

3. Never place a purse on the seat in a convertible or sedan. Put it on the floor or under the seat.

4. Avoid traveling alone.

5. Avoid back streets that are unlit, especially when traveling alone. Attackers very seldom look for victims where witnesses abound.

6. Pleasant smiles are very nice to give and receive but, when giving a gift, be quite sure that the receiver is not receiving more than you intended. Remember that people often read what they want to see into a gesture.

7. When parking in any public place, never park away from the normal flow of traffic. Victims are usually victims when there are no witnesses.

8. Again, when Jane went into the hills, she was out and alone. There are a lot of deranged men that believe when a woman makes herself vulnerable in so many ways she is looking for trouble.

Men, women, the elderly and the very young must avoid any situation that could put them in jeopardy. People must realize that there are thousands of people that live with the devil in their hearts. These people can honestly make themselves believe that a victim deserved what they got.

Remember back to your school days, to the kids that seemed to be picked on the most. They were the ones that let it get to them. They reacted strongly to criticism or teasing. They were the first to show tears and run for cover. They went around with downcast eyes and tended to stay to themselves.

Because they reacted to the teasing in a way that gratified the teaser and since they posed no threat to their teasers they were the ones other kids picked on. The more they were picked on the more they withdrew to themselves.

Well, those bullies are still around today, only now they are looking for something other than ego gratification. As adults themselves, they no longer look to their own age group or younger for victims. But they still look for those same signs of withdrawal, meekness, and vulnerability.

Go out into a public place. Stand off to one side and watch the people as they pass through several areas. Go to a parking lot late at night. (Be careful not to seem to be a threat, or perhaps the police could become interested in your actions.) Go to a public sidewalk, and watch the people. You will find that certain types of people seem to stand out as vulnerable. The obvious ones are the little old ladies or men, barely able to keep their heads up, and the sickly looking child. Others seem to take on a more subtle air of vulnerability with such characteristics as downcast eyes, a slouched posture, not being able to meet passers-by with eye contact. Tidiness seems to be a minor factor. The well-dressed, smart-looking person seems to be capable of "command decisions and actions." Perhaps it's more their attitude than their dress that gives them that appearance. As you watch, the passers by will begin to fit into patterns. By their appearance you may be able to recognize weakness or timidity; you may see the vulnerability that so many thieves look for, perhaps only instinctively.

Quite often we can avoid trouble by following some simple guidelines:

1. Walk with purpose in your step. Stand up tall, step out.
2. Maintain eye-level contact with a passer-by.
3. When threatened with a possible aggressive act maintain a calm, firm, outward appearance.
4. Never aggravate the problem by showing anger.

PROFESSIONAL DEFENSES

There are many people who believe that because of social and economic conditions they need to protect themselves as professionals would protect themselves. The difficulty with that belief is that, even though they may have the need, they probably won't have the ability to obtain and maintain the necessary skills.

Police and the military are trained in many forms of defense. They can use nightsticks, karate, judo and other forms of physical defense and aggression. They spend months acquiring these skills and they maintain them with hours of practice as well as with on-the-job use. The layperson, on the other hand, even if he acquires these abilities, does not maintain them to a peak of ability required for effectiveness. A person cannot rely on an all-but-forgotten skill that no longer really exists. Actually, unused skills become more liability than asset since that person would probably take more chances or become more aggressive than the average person simply because he has overestimated his own abilities. One of the first issues a layperson should recognize is his shortcomings. Secondly, he should recognize his abilities.

For any professional or layperson, skills in self-defense must be acquired in the following order. To deviate from or to skip any one of these skills in order to acquire one further down is definitely inadvisable.

Self-Confidence

Three-hundred-pound football players don't do well in professional basketball. The football player doesn't have the sprinting stamina, he is not adept at shooting baskets or in avoiding contact instead of making contact. If you provide security measures within the perimeters of your ability, you will be very confident playing your own game. Create a game that you can play.

Physical Fitness

Physical stamina is a very important issue. If you can run one to ten miles without stopping all of your physical abilities will be enhanced. Not one soldier or policeman goes into combat or police work without having the physical stamina to cope with the job. If someone hits you, you can't shoot or stab him: you must be capable of fighting or running. If you can't win, give up; don't fight a person for the sake of a few valuables.

Personal Combat Skills

Combat skills may be those gained from a three-hour course in vulnerable attack points on up to a Black Belt in karate or judo. Anything other than a basic knowledge of boxing or attack points requires extensive training as well as continuing practice. I don't think the average person will have the time or interest to acquire combat skills. These skills require many months of training and practice and probably lie outside the realm of reality for most people. Therefore, I would suggest that everyone attend basic classes in self-defense. Keep classes to a minimum such as two evenings of instruction. If you feel compelled to go beyond that, attend classes in your local area. Don't try to learn personal combat skills out of a book. Repetition and classroom environment are necessary for competence. Keep in mind that possession and use of blackjacks, billy clubs, nunchakus, and any other blunted instruments made to kill or maim is against the law in most states.

CS and CN Gas

There are a lot of nonlethal weapons on the market. The one that is recommended to most people is CS gas or mace (CN gas). CS gas is not the well-known mace or CN gas. CS gas is reportedly ten times more effective than CN. In actual tests, a victim of CS gas experiences extreme pain, a choking sensation, and difficulty breathing. Further, when the gas fumes enter the victim's eyes, he is unable to open them for a period of time. Gas canisters come in many sizes and shapes ranging from the size of a fist pack to large bottles. The gas is propelled from nine to fifteen feet through the air.

The proponents of CS gas say that CS is ten times stronger than CN and that it lasts longer. The proponents of CN say CS sometimes takes as much as a minute to take effect. I personally will carry CS gas because I want as much time as possible to get out of harm's way.

Gas Tactics

First I want to tell you when *not* to use gas:
1. Never demonstrate the use of gas by squirting someone.
2. Never try to hold someone at bay with the gas.

3. Do not think gas is a match for a gun or knife.
4. After squirting someone with gas, never stick around.
5. Don't be thrifty. If you use the smaller gas container once, replace it.
6. Don't use gas on the offensive; use it only in self-defense.
7. Keep gas away from children. In some states it is a crime to give gas to a juvenile.
8. Never leave gas lying around.

Consider the gas as a close-in equalizer. If an aggressor hits you or is in any way threatening bodily harm, it becomes your option to equalize the situation or neutralize the aggressor. Consider the gas as a light switch. When you hit your aggressor with the gas in his face and eyes, you have put out his lights but your aggressor could still grope around in the dark and do you damage. Some people will be able to carry out their hostility even after being hit so get away from the aggressor very quickly.

At the very least always follow these suggestions:

1. Carry the canister in your hand, especially when you are in a darkened parking lot or walking down a deserted street.
2. When you carry the canister in your hand for protection, flip the safety catch off.
3. After squirting someone, leave the area immediately and call the police.
4. Carry your gas on your key chain if possible. Your keys also can be used as a weapon.
5. Always squirt in the face and eyes. The gas does not have any effect unless there is face and eye contact.
6. Always carry it with you.

Be careful: gas is a nonlethal weapon, but it is still a weapon. Use it only when needed and respect it for what it is—a weapon that can cause great pain.

Guns

Guns are the most misunderstood defensive weapon in our society. Almost everyone believes that all they have to do to be safe is to have a gun. "If I have a gun, I can protect my family and friends whenever a bad guy comes after them." That's fallacy I hope to dispel.

Legally, in almost all states, a person can shoot a gun at another person only if his life or another's life is being threatened. Further, most states have laws against even the brandishment of weapons in a threatening manner. Keep in mind that most important factor—"life-threatening situation." Before we cover this issue in depth, let's lay some groundwork. Answer the following questions Yes or No.

1. If you find a burglar running out the front door with your color TV, can you shoot him?

2. If you wake up in the middle of the night and a burglar is just leaving your bedroom with a box containing your silver, can you shoot him?

3. If you are run off the road by a passing vehicle and the occupant jumps out of his car after it comes to a stop and comes at you, fists clenched, saying he's going to tear you limb from limb, can you shoot him?

4. If a man breaks in your door after you have told him to go away, and he hits you with his fist three times on the head, breaking your nose, can you shoot him?

I imagine I have been able to stir up your emotions enough to receive a yes answer at least once, although by now you may have realized that all the answers should be No, Maybe, or It depends. There is plenty of case law about burglary where the distinction is made between "life-threatening" and "property-threatening." The burglars in questions 1 and 2 are leaving your presence and pose no threat at that time so you can't shoot. In question 3, the man may have had in mind to kill you by running you off the road, but he didn't and your life is not now threatened by his clenched fists. In question 4, certainly the man is inflicting you with great physical pain, but you can't kill someone because they hurt you. If you believe a person is going to take your life, you have the right to shoot him but how do you get hold of a gun at that point?

The issue concerning when to shoot and when not to shoot can present extreme danger. I have spoken to many district attorneys and police officials on this subject. What they all say, in effect, is, "Well, it's really not that simple. If a person can *prove* his life was threatened, then and only then can the shooting be termed "justifiable." That means we should all consult with an attorney before we shoot and I guess I should recommend just that, but the issue remains quite complicated. For instance, if a little old lady starts beating on a big hulk of a man, he certainly can't shoot, but if the hulk of a man started beating on the little old lady, perhaps she could. The final decision as to when to shoot must be an individual one. I caution you to be aware that there are very few incidents when a person can shoot and not suffer criminal and/or civil retaliation.

When can you shoot: when someone is threatening your life with violence and it appears as if they will succeed; if someone has shot at you or someone else or endangered your life; if you answer your door and someone sticks a gun in your ribs. (It would be a fool's act to try to pull a gun. Better to not open the door to strangers.)

Which Gun

I hope that I have talked you out of using a gun in 99.9 percent of the possibilities. Perhaps now you will consider the use of a gun under the proper circumstances.

First of all, handguns are *out*. Handguns are used when a person deliberately has to go into a hostile environment, such as when a police officer or other official is performing his duty.

What you require is a defensive weapon for your home. If you live in the city, put aside all high-powered deer guns or magnum guns of any sort. Those guns will probably kill more innocent people than anything else.

The gun I recommend for a city environment to protect your home is a shotgun, preferably a 12-gauge pump with an open or improved cylinder choke. With this weapon people farther away than a hundred yards cannot receive much of an injury. If an attacker is over fifty yards away in a city environment, leave him alone, he may go away. In the country, a high-powered gun could be necessary, but I tend to think not. Even in the country if an attacker is far off he may decide to go away. A deer rifle can kill a neighbor who is a mile away.

If you purchase a gun, receive proper training in its use. Find someone who will train you in hunting techniques. Avoid the person who will train you to kill people. He will only train you to kill fast and maybe wrongly. Besides, a person who trains in aggressive techniques usually trains a person to get his gun out first and take cover second. People who have guns tend to go for the gun rather than for cover.

Keep your gun in your home, high on a gun rack. If it must be kept loaded, be sure that your children can't reach it. Anyone who has guns must make their children aware of the dangers. Unload the gun, let them hold it, and explain to them how dangerous it is. If your children are disobedient and are inclined to do what they please even with instructions to the contrary, *lock up your guns*.

Remington's model 870 is very good. It has a pump action that has never failed me in my ten years of use. When the first round is fired, and with a slight pull to the rear, the action almost opens automatically. Further, it is less likely to jam than any other model. There are several different sizes of chokes to choose from. I believe that an improved cylinder is the only choice.

Chapter Four

SECURITY IN HARD TIMES

THE STEERING COMMITTEE

When times become much harder you will have an advantage if your neighborhood has been actively involved in a passive watch program for some time. The steering committee should have learned to cope with one another and with basic problems during their growing pains. If you have not had the steering committee or the home security in progress at all, by all means go back to prior chapters and start there. It will serve no useful purpose to skip the basics and jump right into the more severe measures without the work and preplanning necessary to secure your individual home.

It is also necessary to recognize your responsibilities to your family, your neighborhood, and your society. Just because you have decided to create your own security in a hostile environment does not mean that you will now stand away from society, apart from its rules and regulations. Quite the contrary is true: if your program is to work in troubled times you must stand out as a pillar of just and moral action. If and when a group such as yours steps across that line of moral activity, it opens the door to many forms of trouble.

First and foremost, your community must not abandon your group. The neighborhood group will work only as well as the assistance you receive from the community. One neighborhood will not do as well as two neighborhoods. Alienation of others at this point could create an outcast climate that could put you in extreme jeopardy. Self-help and cooperation are the most important qualities your group will need.

I don't know exactly what is going to occur—in Appendix A are writers who seem to know—but I do know that now is the time for preparation. If you have a year's supply of food and a shortage occurs, yours will be one family fewer that will have to be supplied with a shortened food supply. There are many books to tell you how to store food and goods you will need for hard times (see Appendix B). I will show you how to protect them without using violence as your first line of defense.

Remember one important factor about some of the people in our society today: when their children are starving, they won't sit idly by and let it happen. Many people will take advantage of others who are not prepared and even some who are.

I will provide you with design modifications and measures that could secure your home in a socially and morally unsure era. The threat of an active defense of your property is necessary to secure your home: an aggressor has to believe that you would defend your property—with violence if necessary. The measures I suggest will tell a potential assailant or thief, "Keep away from here. I am prepared." Your steering committee will, as a unit, be more capable of putting that message across.

Add the following responsibilities to your committee in this approximate order:

1. Dealing with the police
2. Neighborhood active patrol
3. Closed security system: gates and guard house
4. Alarm procedures
5. Communications
6. Active defense
7. Cooperative construction: observation points, windows, porches, dog runs, fencing

POLICE

Dealing with the police in times of massive inflation or depression may be a very touchy situation. You must understand what the situation will be: the police will be dealing with riots at supermarkets because of food shortages and possible riotous behavior at city hall, when people are without lights, water, and food. Further, because of the many people who were not prepared, there will be a large increase of burglaries, robberies, and all other violent crimes. The police will be arresting their neighbors, in some instances, for creating public panic or for stealing from someone who had what they needed. In short, the police officer is going to look upon all of you who are prepared as potential offenders.

The officer most likely will look upon you as a hoarder, and very possibly as a likely cause of the problems, only because you were prepared. For that reason and many others, never let anyone, including your committee, know the location of your food or other storage. Acquire your goods prior to these difficult times and be able to prove, in writing, that you did. If you don't have proof that you purchased the food prior to the shortage a police officer could arrive with a warrant, search and seize your property, and accuse you of hoarding. You are *not* hoarding if you acquire your food storage prior to the hard times.

You should invite your police department to a steering committee meeting. I can imagine how the police officer might react to this situation if not handled properly. First, he may think that this is just another form of civil disorder he has to attend to. He will also be able to say (maybe to himself) "These people are arming themselves to protect their stores of goods and they want official sanction to shoot someone." The problem is large. Choose someone who knows someone in the police department to act as liaison. If you don't have a person to vouch for you, you'll just have to prove yourself. This means plenty of cooperation with the police department.

Outline your security procedures as they are outlined here, or revise them to suit your needs, but keep them in the realm of reality. Show your concern and willingness to cooperate but remember: the officer's job is also to avoid panic. He may try to pacify you and talk you completely out of your security measures. Do not let him talk you out of securing yourself, but certainly accept his good advice. Ultimately, you and the police are there for the same reason.

Martial law is possible during these bad times. I couldn't possibly prepare you for the authority the police will have then. Be aware of the possibility and stay on their good side.

As time goes on, set up a communications network with the police, as simple as citizens band radios or as elaborate as buying FM radios that are compatible with the department's. If you have to go to CB radios you may be overheard by those you want to be protected against, so be aware.

ACTIVE PATROL

As further improvement on watching your neighbors' homes, form a neighborhood watch patrol, or an active patrol. Many communities have already resorted to this, some quite effectively.

The steering committee will assign patrols made up of people from your neighborhood to drive through the area as a mobile patrol. This system becomes necessary when crime occurs in spite of a passive watch system and the police. Your community should decide on this system at any time a major change occurs in the form of a disaster, hyperinflation, large changes in unemployment, or any major shortage in basic commodities.

The issue is "constructive paranoia." If a potential aggressor sees this activity in the neighborhood, he is more likely to move to another area to do his damage. Do not involve yourself in active searches or in questioning people. Leave that activity to the police.

In the meantime, recognize any unstable people who might try to become part of your group. You'll recognize them by their "strut." They may even have a gun hidden just out of sight. They might stop a car or two and question the occupants just because there wasn't enough action. This type of person might cause more problems than your neighborhood could handle.

Your chairman should be capable of warning these people about unwanted activities and then have the option of removing them from your patrol roster.

Following is a typical situation the patrol might encounter. The patrol might come upon a car parked in the neighborhood. The patrol, which should consist of a car marked PATROL or NEIGHBORHOOD PATROL, should pass by the subjects at least twice while writing down the license number of the car. The patrol should then park facing the subjects and watch them from at least a block away. If they determine the subjects are no threat at all, they could drive up and confirm that fact. If the subjects do not move, the patrol would activate prearranged signals recognized in the neighborhood. The patrol would honk the horn three times which would signal the neighborhood to look out and turn on their floodlights and give a short blast on their horns. The patrol would, at the same time, call the police.

Put yourself in the thieve's position. You and your friends drive into a neighborhood you intend to steal from. There is nowhere to hide close to the houses—everything has been cleared out—so you sit in your car and look the neighborhood over. You intend to steal from the most prosperous-looking house and use guns to get whatever they may have—food, gold, money, etc. While you are sitting there discussing the options with your group, this private car drives by twice. On its side is a magnetic sign: PATROL. There are two people inside, a man and a woman. The patrol then parks down the street facing you. After about two minutes, the house you are sitting in front of turns on several large lights. If this isn't bad enough, the patrol car honks a loud horn three times, waits a minute, and honks three more times. All of a sudden the neighborhood lights up like a Christmas tree, first one house and then another, until all front security lights are on. At the same time, the inside lights in the homes go off. In addition, horns from the other houses start sounding with a short blast. At this point, what do you do? Well, in my opinion, after such a display only the most foolhardy thief or criminal will try to do anything other than run.

These tactics are not going to catch many crooks, but they will probably prevent someone from becoming one, at least in your neighborhood. In the end, your property is safe and your neighborhood becomes known as secure. Criminals will probably pick on the unfortunate area that has not prepared itself.

The patrol should have the option of relaying messages to the residents through the radio communication system. This would be necessary to determine whether strangers are a possible threat. If the patrol calls the base station, and they put through a call to the home where the strangers are parked, it should be easy to identify the strangers as friends or as a possible threat. The resident could then turn on the outer security lights, if at night, prior to sounding an alarm.

If the police are not able to respond because of civil disorders, riots, or other more menacing reasons, it may be necessary to blockade the streets or install a closed security system.

CLOSED SECURITY SYSTEM

A closed security system is used now in apartment complexes, high-rise apartments, and in some exclusive neighborhoods. The idea is simple: close off all access to the area by fences and walls except for one entrance operated by guards and a gate. If this technique becomes necessary, it would be best to uniform your guards and possibly even arm them. Keep in mind, though, that you may need a state license and permits to carry weapons. You may also have to contend with even stricter laws involving gun control. But, as a bare minimum, local police should sanction such activity.

If a gate watch is necessary, your manpower needs will increase. Have at least two people on the gate and two people on patrol. Constant communications should be maintained between the gate and the mobile unit, with quick switch-over to the police channels.

During hard times, and if your neighborhood is financially well off, it might be to your advantage to hire personnel, but remember that you may be hiring the thieves you are trying to protect against. They may take such a job to have access to your valuables. Also, any person you may hire would not have a vested interest in protecting you and your family and, therefore, may leave at the first sign of real trouble. Who can blame him? No job is worth a hole in the chest. So it may fall back again to the residents and local law enforcement.

If at all possible have a route by which the patrol can drive all the way around the area. This may be a weak link if not covered through visual access. Removing the fencing in backyards and between houses may enhance your security by giving your patrol greater access to watch the rear of the houses. Under extreme circumstances the property-line fence would remain, but eight-foot openings at the edge of the property line should be cleared to enable a car to pass through back yards. The yards could then be fenced, shortening the back yard but giving the necessary access, on the order of alleyways. Access routes should be placed throughout the back yard alley so that the patrol may gain access to the main road whenever the need arises.

There are alternatives to back yard patrol such as putting dog runs in out-of-the-way places. This is also a good deterrent but still requires additional fencing. (See our section on guard dogs.)

Gates

In the event of extreme social and economic problems, gates and fencing will be necessary to close off your neighborhood to outsiders. These gates and fences may take the form of cars parked across the roadways or hastily erected chain-link fencing. What form this takes depends on many things. Among them:

How much time is available before the need is present
Availability of materials
Availability of funds to finance such a venture

The issue becomes a matter of doing the best with what you have. If you have plenty of time and money you may decide to use the following system.

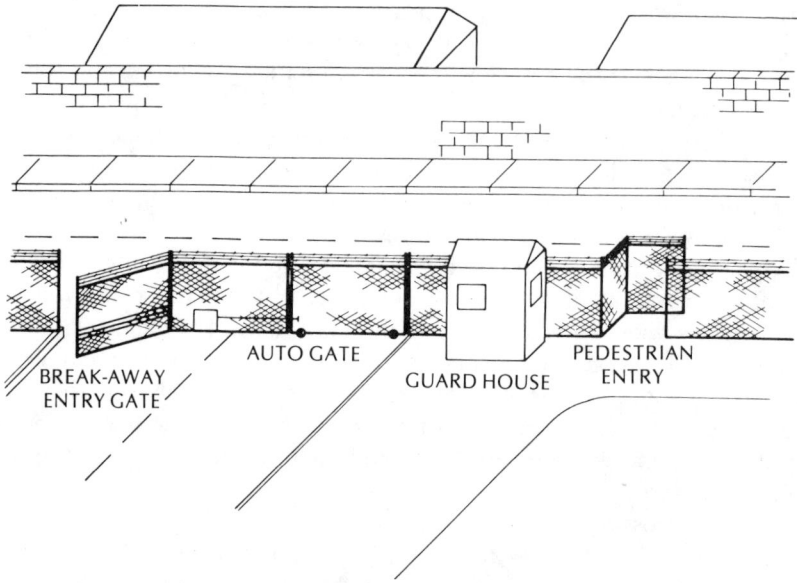

BREAK-AWAY ENTRY GATE   AUTO GATE   GUARD HOUSE   PEDESTRIAN ENTRY

The gates, ideally, should be of the single-slide-roller type. This gate rolls back on wheels; it does not have to swing out and into the roadway. It can be controlled either by a lock and key or by a remote control station located in the guardhouse. The gate should be made of chain-link fencing with multiple reinforcement throughout. Barbed wire strands should be on top of the fencing.

There should be several bumper mounds on the road before the entrance to slow down any vehicle entering the neighborhood. Next to the regular entrance should be a gate not normally used. Design this gate with a bumper that will break and swing open on its hinges with the pressure of three hundred pounds. This will enable the police to enter regardless of what may be blocking the normal drive.

There should also be a pedestrian gate. This could take several forms, although the most likely would be an overlapping fence. This fence should have a normal opening and on one side should be a portion of fence that extends out at a 90-degree angle for about two feet. The extended piece should turn back another 90 degrees to completely cover the exit. This will enclose the entrance so that a person cannot ride a motorbike or any other type of vehicle through the entrance. It would further prevent masses of people rushing the area without being slowed down. Ideally, the gate should be placed on the opposite side of the guardhouse from the automobile gate and should have the capability of being locked when necessary.

Guardhouse

When civil disorders reach their height, you will require a vantage point from which two people can control your neighborhood entrance. This vantage point will enable two people to stand guard at your front gate with limited risk. The vantage point can take many forms, such as a trailer or other autos parked ten yards from the fence and gate. It could be a part of one of the houses or just a sandbagged wall erected to observe the traffic as it comes and goes.

Any changes such as these must blend well so that your neighborhood does not stand out as the one with the most to protect. In this period people will be banding together for their mutual defense. Drawing undue attention to yourself could be quite dangerous.

The ideal construction would be a guardhouse that could withstand even the most severe assault. The house should be constructed on the property line of a corner residence. This street corner will be the only entrance to your neighborhood. The house should be constructed of brick reinforced with steel and filled with concrete. Bulletproof glass should be used in all windows used to observe surrounding areas. The door should be constructed of ¼-inch steel and set in a steel frame. The roof must have the capability of withstanding considerable impact. Contained within the guardhouse should be a radio to communicate with the roving patrol and a radio to contact the police. The neighborhood intercom should also extend to this building.

The automobile gate should be controlled by the guard at his post. All residents should have additional access to the gate by other means, such as an external-keyed gate control.

COMMUNICATIONS

A primary concern for any group of people who are actively involved in establishing a security system should be providing for adequate communications. This can be done using something as simple as CB radios or with more elaborate systems such as a business band radio. Citizens' band radio should be considered only as a last resort because the criminal element today now uses the CB radio for its own purpose. They will post lookouts to notify themselves of potential trouble. If you are using these radios you must be aware that your communications may be overheard.

The most practical form of communications is an intercom system installed in each residence. The intercom should be placed either in the family room or in the living room, but it must be in the room with your front yard observation point. The intercom should always be left on and used only for emergency measures so that when an alarm is sounded everyone in the neighborhood will know exactly what is confronting them. The committee chairman can further direct operations concerning tactics and the chairman should relay information on the status of the problem.

Intercom systems installed should have an amplifier so that the most distant call can be heard. The intercom wires can be run from house to house at little expense. The system should also be usable on an auxiliary power system, such as a bank of 12-volt batteries or a generator. A further phoning procedure can be used to call the police.

An additional system should be available for use in your patrol cars. Again, this could be citizens' band radios but you would probably be better off with business band radios. Your objective should be to have a direct communication route to your residence without having to leave the patrol car. The patrol should be able to contact the base station who would, in turn, contact the residence in question.

The scenario could go something like this:

The patrol car, while driving down the street, spots a car parked on the road. As the patrol passes, heads drop below the windows. There are probably two people in the front seat. Upon seeing this, the patrol car calls the base station radio who in turn calls the house where the car is parked. The base station learns that the daughter is still out on a date and is probably one of the occupants of the car. When this is learned, either Dad can go out and ask his daughter to come in or the patrol can pull up and ask the driver to identify himself. If the people are unknown, the resident could turn on his outer floodlights (not awakening the neighborhood) prior to sounding his alarm. The lights coupled with the patrol car activity should create an environment where any nonaggressive persons would leave without further action. If the car does not leave a blast from your horn could follow.

ACTIVE DEFENSE

Active defense may be the most touchy procedure of your security program. If your neighbor is being beaten, robbed, raped, or plundered, it is very difficult for anyone to sit back and wait for the police. All the more reason to sit down with the committee and think this out before the actual problem occurs. Your committee should consider consequences and alternatives long before such an emotionally charged moment actually occurs.

Certainly, response time for the police should be carefully analyzed by the steering committee, and if police consistently arrive within a short time the problem should be left to them. In the meantime, if large floodlights come on throughout the neighborhood so that there is nowhere for potential aggressors to hide, they should leave very quietly.

But what if aggressors have already entered the victim's home and have control of the victim? Rushing in or any act of aggression may be lethal for the victim as well as for people who are trying to help. The best thing to do at this point is to give the thief or assailant a way out and wait for the police. Try to avoid trouble before it gets to a point where shooting is a possibility. Even if the police are responding slowly, it is still best to wait. Anyone held captive can only be hurt by your aggression.

OBSERVATION POINTS

It is most essential for you to be able to observe your front and back yards without being seen. From such an observation point you should be able to turn on the outer floodlights as you sound your alarm system. Your observation point should also contain any personal protection devices that you may deem necessary.

It is best not to use a window for an observation point. A window will expose you and your family to the possibility of direct assault. If your living room is in the front of your house, it is the best place for an observation point. Use a corner about the height of your shoulders. Make your observation port no larger than is necessary but it should be at least half a square foot. Use tinted bulletproof or safety glass. Have a second opening facing any possible hiding areas in your yard. These ports will offer you visibility to the front yard as well as the side of your property. in fact, the side port may overlook your front porch. The same is true for your back yard and the same lighting systems and alarms must be set up at a point in back of the house.

WINDOWS

Windows can be protected from a juvenile burglar by many means (most discussed in a prior chapter). There are locking devices that can secure them well. In this section we are concerned with more aggressive situations.

First, wrought-iron bars can be used to keep burglars out. Make sure the bars have a release mechanism for at least one window in each room. The release device will let anyone on the inside get out in case of fire or other emergency.

Wrought-iron bars will not keep a professional burglar out; they will only discourage the less-prepared thief. All the thief needs is a large pair of bolt cutters. The bars give little or no resistance. Be aware that people who use wrought iron have a false sense of security and often leave their burglar alarm off. On hot days they may even leave their windows partially open after a time without any trouble. Don't fall into that trap.

Second, installation of shutters all the way around the house could become mandatory. They should be made of at least two-inch-thick wood, reinforced with metal plating. These shutters can be made of two sheets of one-inch plywood glued together with a metal plate glued inside. Strategic windows should have a port within the shutter. These should be placed toward the lower portion of the shutter and should open inward. They should be at least three inches high and twelve inches long. These ports should be held together with durable wrought-iron hinges that close with a bolt.

Whichever you choose, make sure the shutters are locked from inside and that they open outward. They must open with a bolt or a hasp and they should not require keys. You must be able to release them quickly without fumbling for keys.

Hinge your shutters with large wrought-iron hinges that, when closed, offer no means of unbolting. They can be secured by welding your outside bolts to the hinge or by using rounded bolt heads. Be able to use your windows as an escape route. I do not know that anyone will ever be put in the position of actively defending their home against violence, but if we go through these times shuttering will be necessary.

Front-yard picture windows are another problem. You can use bars but I think it will be necessary to close them off completely. The ideal way would be to build a wall around picture windows. The wall should be as high as your eaves and on one side you should have a locked gate for access. This would enable you to gain access and have a patio or at least to have plants for a picturesque setting.

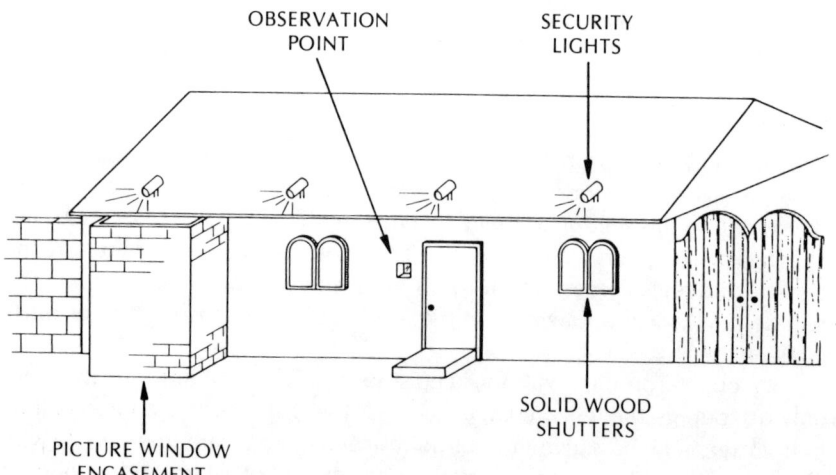

PORCHES

Porches in homes are nearly always recessed from the leading edge of the home. They are good places for a thief to hide from observers but they can be effectively walled in and used for a double-door entry system.

The ultimate porch security is to have a door which can be unlocked by remote control. When an unknown person rings your bell, the automatic device unlocks the outer door and lets him in. When he enters he will find himself in a porch area and confronted by a second door. Now he is in an enclosed area, unable to get out. You will be able to look him over carefully before you make any decision. If you think he is a threat, simply call the police or the patrol. This means that any window or any other access to the house must be closed to him. At the very least you can go to your new front door and investigate, even though there is no electronic lock. If the potential aggressor gets in, the only access he will have is to you and your front porch. He still has another solid door to get through in order to get to your family.

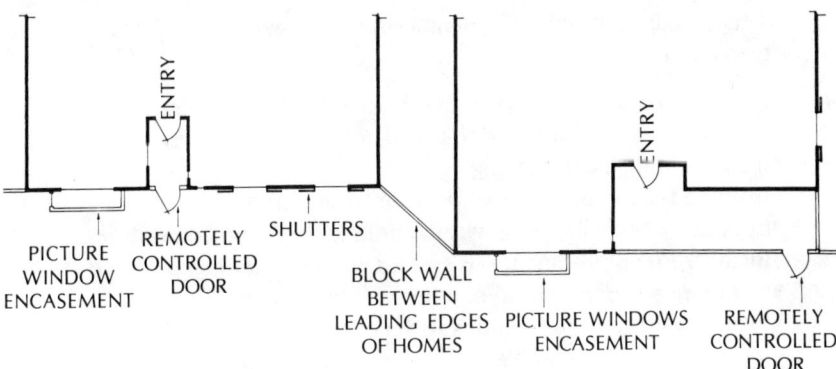

EDUCATION OF OTHERS

The most secure neighborhood will be in the most secure town. If you have the chance (and you should actively pursue it) you should try to help other neighborhoods in your area. There are many good people out there. They may have the same goals in mind as you have but they may not have the knowledge or experience you will have. Give them help. Invite responsible people to your meetings and create an environment of self-help and cooperation.

I believe that the larger the area that is secure, the more secure your neighborhood will become. Don't increase your area by neighborhood after neighborhood, spreading your patrols thinner. Help other neighborhoods to start their own program. Keep to the basic neighborhood security concept and try not to increase your area unless times get much better years down the road.

There will probably be those in your neighborhood who either don't believe the measures are needed or who may be too scared to become involved. Try to understand that some people can't handle stress and problems of this nature. Be patient. Once they see the light they will probably come around. When they do, bring them up-to-date and make them welcome.

TIMING FOR HARD TIMES

The following conditions may give you some indication about when to go to the second stage of preparedness discussed in this chapter.

- When riots occur within thirty miles of your home
- When inflation rate exceeds 25 percent
- When unemployment exceeds 12 percent
- When a major natural catastrophe occurs
- When minor shortages occur in basic commodities
- When bank holidays occur

In these cases, bring your neighborhood together and enhance your security even further:

- Enact an active patrol system with your neighborhoods' help
- Install sensors in your yard that will notify you of a person's presence
- Install leading-edge fencing
- Install a second door enclosing your front porch
- Conduct weekly meetings with your neighborhood committee
- Install your communications system within your neighborhood
- Install means of communications with the police
- Install radio communications with your patrol
- Install observation points in the front and back of your home
- Educate others

If riots occur in your city, if food vanishes from the store shelves, or if a major disaster occurs there may not be much time to act. In fact, at this point, the chances are very slim that you will be able to acquire fencing materials, electronic locks (if you have electricity at all) or other materials suggested in this book. If possible, take the following measures and any other measures your committee may deem necessary:

- Install shutters on your home
- Install a closed security system
- Put up gates and some manner of concealment for your guards
- Put dog runs in out-of-the-way places (Perhaps acquire additional large dogs from a pound)
- Have your outer doors reinforced with steel plating
- Fireproof your property to the best of your ability

You must preplan. You must be aware of the coming of hard times and be ready when they come. If you can afford finer, more expensive measures now, by all means install them. If you are on a limited budget make your money count. Items bought by the whole neighborhood may only mean a few dollars to you personally. Purchase those items that make you independent and secure. Don't buy intercoms, for example, if your neighborhood is not working with you.

In the final analysis, I can only guide you in timing on a limited basis. Don't panic and draw undue attention to yourselves. Don't be too late and open yourselves up to jeopardy. Be aware of the "Fort Knox" problem. If your house becomes a fortress among the unprepared, you are the obvious target. You will appear as the one with something to guard. Make your changes in a subtle way over a period of time. Start now and work smoothly. Change you must, but with small strokes, not with an exaggerated abandon.

APARTMENT COMPLEXES

Living in a dwelling where your only living area is indoors is very defensible, but your chances of self-reliance are decreased. There is always a trade-off — one part security for one part self-sufficiency. This is certainly true in apartments as well. The apartment dweller will find it harder to grow or raise what they may need during these times.

Apartments, whether they are high-rise buildings or complexes, are very defensible. An apartment building or complex is a high-density area with no place where a person can come in and not be seen, if your job of defense is done properly. Further, there is a very small area to be protected in proportion to the number of people there to protect it.

Apartments can be defended and secured if certain concepts are understood.

First, you are relying on the capable assistance of the neighborhood patrol and the local police. Most of the same concepts and techniques apply here as in residential security.

Second, as in the neighborhood security situation, you will always be setting up a climate where the thief is going to have to say, "There are easier pickings down the street, so why mess with these people?"

Fencing

Fencing around your perimeter must be a block wall at least seven feet high, topped with two feet of wrought-iron metalwork with points. Don't make it easy. Behind the wall, and at intervals of fifty yards, platforms should be constructed that will enable the patrol to see over the wall without much jeopardy. Army surplus periscope devices may be a beneficial option. But don't put holes in the walls: if you can see out, aggressors can see in.

It is important to look formidable. You want the appearance of security for your apartment: even more secure than the apartments down the street. People will look on this and say, "Well the owner is selling security at his apartments, but the people inside may not have any more than we do." I think there is a noticeable difference between a single-residence show of fortification and an apartment-complex's show of fortifications.

Perhaps your landlord would agree to the fencing idea if the tenants in the apartment complex agreed to pay an additional one hundred dollars a month to compensate him for the cost of the improvements.

Follow the steps of security already recommended for residences for a passive and active patrol and also for a closed security system.

Closed Security System for Apartments

For a high-rise it's simple: cover up your glass and install secondary doors so you hold entering people captive while you look them over. In the sprawling apartment complex, the wall-and-gate system is necessary. There should be two sets of gates: the tenant enters one, it closes, and he enters the second and goes home.

Any external parking should also be a part of your security system. If a high-rise has underground parking, it is a matter of closing off entrances and exits with the double-exit system. Always use the double-entry system: the psychological trauma of your potential aggressor having to enter an area where he is kept captive at the dweller's will is in itself quite a deterrent.

There should be at least four people on a shift: two on patrol and two for the gate or door. If you choose to have two separate entrances you must provide more manpower.

For sprawling apartment complexes, it is absolutely necessary to have a driveable road around the perimeter and along the wall. There should be a means of communicating an alarm to the residents. There also has to be normal lighting throughout the area with additional lighting to be used in case of an alarm. (See Cooperative Construction in Chapter Two.)

Each resident should be capable of responding, as in Chapter Two. Keep in mind the psychological factors of the plan: not just two or four guards, but the whole neighborhood is going to rise up.

You are in a better position to defend yourself if you have an active program in progress. But you must cover the basics: you must eliminate hiding places; you must have total cooperation of residents; and you must have good communications; and, further, the potential thief must believe that behind all of this might possibly be violence in the form of police or other forceful means.

Chapter Five

RURAL OR FARM SECURITY

For several hundred years, 15- to 20-foot-high walls surrounded by a moat filled with crocodiles saved many a castle from the pillages of a roving band of ruffians. Townships came into being because the farmers banded together to erect strongholds of mutual defense. They built villages guarded by walls made from 15-foot-high spiked logs, with walkways and bunkers from which to fight. Our western frontiers were marked by forts, complete with towers, to combat the rampages of the Indian.

As times become harder, a home or hideaway away from the normal flow of traffic will be extremely vulnerable. Imagine a group of people who are in need of what a farm has to offer.

Three men who are out to get what they can—and who don't care what they do to get it—come across a home stuck out in the middle of nowhere. This home could be in farmland, among the pines, or in a hidden valley away from everything. The three men hide their car, pull out shotguns and rifles, and walk to the farm. (For the purpose of our example we will use a very exaggerated dwelling, such as a castle.) As they walk up the road they come upon a clearing. In this clearing is a rather large dwelling with fifteen-foot-high walls. Inside the walls is another courtyard wall, even higher. Their first thought is, "We'll never get in," but they decide it might be worthwhile to stick around and see what they can see. About that time, as they look across a field, they see a man tending some livestock in pens. There are several pens, some with pigs and some with cattle. The man heads back to the castle and, after knocking, enters the large door. Waiting for a minute, the marauders decide this is worth another look, so they get up and make a mad dash to the gate, apparently unobserved. No alarm sounded and no shouts from inside. There is no way to get up the wall and the gate seems firmly in place, so there is apparently no way to get in. A man's voice rings out, "Marge, hurry up, I'm hungry."

Marge, her husband, and their family are no more. All the marauders did was wait for her husband to come out the next morning. They disarmed him, then traced his steps into the very formidable castle.

My point is very simple: there is safety in numbers. If someone had been on the walls patrolling, perhaps these marauders would not have been successful. There are many factors that create security. Most require manpower. Manpower is protection and protection has to be literal as well as implied.

Security in a rural section is going to require more preparation than that of any other environment. What follows is a thumbnail sketch of the most sophisticated security for the lone farmhouse.

ULTIMATE SECURITY

Now with our "thumbnail" in hand, let's take a drive up the road to a maximum-security rural home (see drawing, p. 73). At a right angle off the main highway is a dirt road, rugged and not maintained, traveling off into the woods. A hundred feet down the road our car passes through a photoelectric beam that crosses it. Fifty yards further is an electromagnetic sensor buried in the ground. There is now chain-link fencing paralleling the road on both sides—nothing spectacular, just six feet high and no barbed wire. Two hundred yards further the road turns back on itself in a large circle.

At the back and on both sides are signs stating, "Keep Out, Private Property," but no breaks in the fence. Still further back are three gates, each with call boxes, one on each side of the road. Perhaps there is another gate a hundred yards in from the main road, also with a call box. Each call box and gate is the same. If we were able to get ourselves inside the first gate, we would probably come across the half-wild boar the owner lets run loose in about ten acres of woods.

One of the two gates leads to about fifteen acres of ground, all fenced with two rows of wire fencing, complete with razor-barb tangle lying between them. Both have dirt roads to lead back to the starting point while the third leads to a concrete building. All three gates have numerous photoelectric beams and electromagnetic sensors as well as closed-circuit TVs.

If we had tried to walk in, we would have approached either the wooded area, with the boar, or the road that turned back on itself. Or, if we had tried to go around all the fences, we would find the steep sides of a mountain with what appears to be a lot of refuse from rock slides.

But we went to the right gate and got in by breaking the lock. The area is heavily wooded. There are trees and stumps planted (or perhaps just buried) in every space available that a car could normally drive, to keep the cars on the road. We drive out of the woods by coming out of a turn into a pasture on a gentle slope and we proceed up to a brick house. The house is really quite small, about 750 square feet, topped by a tile roof. There are six windows with metal plates and slits and a metal door tightly closed. A voice sounds out from the speakers on the roof. "Turn around and get out of here, or else." Now where are we? Are there three or thirty guns behind the bunker windows? Is this military or private? Are they killers like us, or are they weak people? Whoever they are, they are prepared.

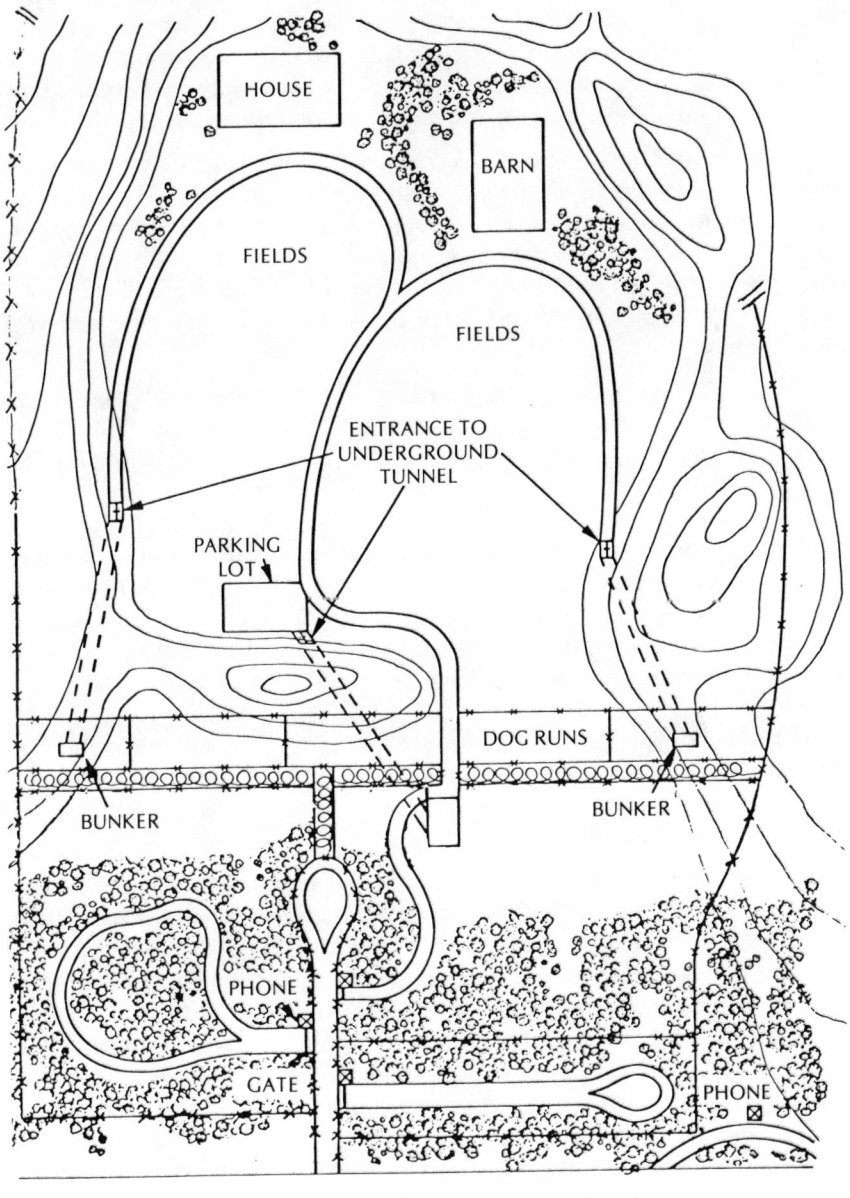

ULTIMATE SECURITY

Now go back to the same place as a resident. You will be heading home after a long day trading with the neighbors. Set back on the highway, and about fifty yards down the road, there is a turnout. Nothing much, just a dirt road that goes off the main highway about twenty yards. About two-thirds of the way into the turnout is a concealed hand phone. You pick up the phone and listen for someone to answer. Someone finally answers and tells you there is no one in any of the trap areas, so you proceed.

You drive to the right gate and enter. (You know that if someone were chasing you, you could hit the gate with your car and it would fling open.) Just then you hear a loud voice (through a hidden speaker), "Someone just turned in," so you drive in but you are very careful not to stir up much dust. You proceed up the road and drive behind the bunker through a narrow, one-car gate. Someone in the bunker opens the automatic gate and you drive through.

Over the crest of the hill is a parking area. The area is in a depression safely out of sight. Since you are a part of this community and, in fact, the only adult male, you get out of the car and go to a small concrete bunker and push the buzzer. Your son comes on the intercom and you identify yourself. The electric lock buzzes and you go into the bunker. You are now walking through a tunnel that ends up at the brick house on the other side of the hill. As you enter the bunker your son says, "There are two men in the area in a convertible jeep. They are in with the hogs now, but they are leaving fast. Mom is on the com and said they have been drinking and have guns." The com sounds and you hear your wife's voice saying, "They just busted the main gate and are on their way. They have passed the middle point and are driving fast. You should see them soon." As you see them, your wife says, "I see them now. What are you going to do?" You say, "Well, we have done it before. We'll do the same as always: call out to turn around and then two warning shots."

It doesn't stop there. Most of your lower land is wasted in traps and electrical wiring. There is further coaxial cable, high in the trees and buried in the ground. Beyond your defensive bunker all along the valley floor is a wrought-iron fence topped with razor wire. Just beyond that fence is a razor-wire tangle stretching the entire length of the valley and there is another chain-link fence just beyond that. At both ends of the valley are defensive bunkers that can be entered at the bunker or from a secret hiding place. Further, about fifty yards beyond the main bunker and just past your parking area, is another chain-link fence. This fence also stretches across the valley and also has additional dividing fencing that sections off the area. In the sectioned-off areas and your parking area are your dogs. There are twelve dogs, three in each section. There's not much more to your security except a few land mines, cameras, and a house that is built like your bunkers. In the main house, the only difference will be that kids, chickens, dogs, and goats are roaming around the area in all but complete security.

Of course your wife is inside six times a day watching the cameras, listening to remote microphones, resetting alarms that were tripped by one thing or another. Your wife does her daily chores closer to the house and can monitor the system when you have to make another mad dash up to the bunkers.

What I have described to you is less than foolproof and a pretty dreary life and of course a band of twenty men, properly equipped, would probably take you, but it is probably the best security you can provide. Further, all of your defenses depend on the potential aggressor not being able to get in from behind.

There is one other problem: cost. It depends on sizes of course, but the structures will range over $100,000; cameras will be $3,000; coaxial cable for the cameras, $5,000; infrared, electromagnetic, and other detectors and the control complex, $10,000; fencing, $15,000; and razor wire, another $10,000. Top all this off with forty chickens, four cows, fifteen guard dogs, three yard dogs, ten pigs, three horses, and you have quite an expense. All of this so that you might be reasonably safe.

If you want self-sufficiency, wouldn't it be nice to have someone at your back to share in the patrolling and the expenses and to give you a great amount of moral support when you really need it? Can you imagine the loneliness—you against the world? Here's the best attempt at a rural cooperative security system.

FARM COMMUNICATION

There is safety in numbers. If the numbers of other people are not close at hand, at least be able to call on them. Set up a CB radio communications network. Have the people in your area, say two square miles, leave their CBs on and tuned to one channel. Have a radio always turned on where you spend the most time—living room, family room, kitchen. If you call for help, and it's there, that means a lot. Your patrol can use the same channel and everyone can sit in on the news. The CB channels are quite often too crowded and you could possibly have to go the FM business band or amateur radio frequencies. Perhaps a channel that is not normally used or a scrambler would work for your CB. You could even string your own telephone line, but that gets expensive. The best thing is to keep your small group in complete communication with each other. Make sure that whatever system you have, you use a speaker system that can be heard at least in the room where you spend the most time, if not in others.

PERIMETER SECURITY

I once visited a small valley in the northern states where, at every property line, there was a solid thicket of blackberries. If you have ever tried to plow your way through blackberries you will know that it's not a pleasant experience. The blackberry bush has a very nasty sticker that almost makes entry impossible. I imagine that those farmers have problems with varmints and insects that breed in the bushes but by thinking in terms of border integrity and good eating, the thicket has pleasant advantages. You should back up the border with chain-link fencing. Don't use brick here: you want to be able to see out. With chain link, you can use binoculars to see what's on the other side.

Fencing

Ideally there should be three fences for your security: one at your border to be breached; the second, fifty yards (twenty-five to fifty yards depending upon your particular needs) away from the main house that shouldn't be breached; and a third, around your house, that can't be breached.

Let's talk about the middle fence, the one fifty yards out. This fence can be used in conjunction with your livestock areas. I don't know of many people who will scuffle with electrified fencing just to confront those nasty boars you use for breeding. Further, people don't usually jump over fences to wrestle with wild dogs, pet bulls, horny rams, and—oh yes—don't forget those nasty geese. They make a terrible racket. The farmyard security force does one very important thing: it gives you time and noise—time to wake up and judge the situation and time to take action.

Now, if someone made his way through your fence and is being chased by those geese (there would be too many to shoot) and all of a sudden floodlights go on and a loud bell sounds, what do you think the intruder is going to do? Perhaps he will decide that he has bitten off more than he can chew and that he should leave before he is the one to get bitten.

If there are no fences on your property now, I believe that the first to be erected should be the one fifty yards out.

Whenever major shortages occur in commodities or jobs, or when any major changes are noticed, the rural property owner should construct the property-line fence. This fence should also be chain link at least six feet high and properly reinforced.

Whenever a substantial portion of the population becomes openly aggressive and ignores the law, a final defensive position should be installed. This position should either be a very defendable house or a fence. If you use a fence, make it close to your house and make it out of concrete block reinforced with steel and filled with concrete. It should be topped with wrought-iron or barbed wire. Go back to the castle construction: make bunkers at the corners. There should be solidly constructed gates at this point. Remember, this is last-chance territory.

Gates

The gates that are used in this security system will vary depending on their position. The gate at the property line—the first gate—should be a normal chain-link-fence gate. The most convenient locking system you can find should be used. If you use padlocks, weld a couple of feet of chain to the lock and then securely fasten the chain to the fence. (Many burglaries have occurred because a thief finds a padlock unlocked and replaces it with his own to be unlocked later.) If a swing-away gate is used make sure that it is solidly constructed and can be made very difficult to enter.

Perhaps, if finances are available, you as farmer or resident should use automatically locking gates—gates that can be made to open by key and to swing closed with a gravity or spring-closing device. A further improvement would be to have electric gates that open and close automatically with the use of a key. This first gate can also have an additional gate adjacent to it, normally locked, that when hit with the bumper of a car will open upon impact. This gate can be necessary if police or your neighbors need to get in to help you.

The second gate will be the most important gate on your property. This gate must be made to withstand the impact of an auto hitting it in an attempt to gain entry. Use hardened steel for this gate and plenty of it. A gate can be defended against a car crashing into it by welding angle iron to the bottom edge of the fence that protrudes out at least three and a half feet toward the outside of the gate. This angle iron should be sharpened to a dull point and must be placed at least every foot along the bottom edge of the gate. Your objective would be to pop the tires of any car trying to crash your gate and thus effectively disable the car. Paint these spikes red or some other very noticeable color; your neighbors might be very upset if they became the victims of this device.

WALL DEFENSE POSITIONS

There should be at least two structures that can be used as wall defense positions. These should be placed at opposite corners of your inner defendable wall. The buildings should be made out of concrete block, filled with concrete. If you can afford it, line the inside of the rooms with ¼-inch steel on walls that face the outside. If you line your walls, add at least an inch of plywood to cover the metal. (This is done to protect you from ricochets.)

The defensive rooms should have slit windows with solidly made shutters that open inward. Those ports should give you visibility of at least one half of your property. The door should be well built and should bolt from the inside. The other room would have a view of the back half of the property.

Inside should be a lighting panel that controls lights, alarms, and any other defensive mechanism. Included in these structures there should also be one high-powered rifle with ammunition. There should also be an intercom system constantly on to enable you to communicate with the other walled room and the house. Construct your walled rooms so that the outward appearance remains the same as your wall. The casual observer should not see a fort but a wall.

HOME CONSTRUCTION

In the farm community, the house will already be there. Perhaps you can help security by adding tile roofing and brick facing around the house. You should have shutters and other items suggested in Chapter Four. You should also have a vantage point from the house from which as much of the terrain as possible can be seen. Those inside the house have to be able to watch all the areas that people in the walled rooms cannot see. For instance, if only husband and wife are available as lookouts, the husband has to be in the walled room while the wife must be able to watch the opposite area. She should be able to operate all of the security devices they could afford to have. In some instances, the husband might want to have controls at the wall as well as in the house.

ALARM SYSTEMS

Probably nearly everyone has seen old war movies where the hero attempts escape from a prison camp by cutting fence wire—all but one alarm wire that breaks the circuit and sounds the alarm. Well, that's what I'm suggesting. Buy cheap wire, send a current through it, and light up a light bulb or sound a buzzer. Most hardware stores have devices that sound a buzzer when electricity goes off. Attach a large bell to that and you have a cheap alarm system.

More sophisticated systems are available, but they are expensive. Sonic, infrared, and photoelectric beams can be used if there are no animals. (See Chapter Two on residential alarms.) Animals can trip most alarms that are sensitive enough to detect a person's presence. (Have you ever heard a cow talk at night or scream when she gets bit by barbed wire?) Microphones placed around your grounds will occasionally give signs of entry. Place a mike in the hidden areas of your property and you may overhear intruders' plans. Better yet, place speakers there as well, and tell them where their plans won't work.

COMMUNITY ROADBLOCKS

Community roadblocks may be a very effective tool during these times. Decide what your borders should be, then place barricades and fencing across as many roads as possible that lead into the neighborhood you are trying to protect.

An ideal solution would be to take advantage of any natural obstructions that may already be there such as canals or large ditches. Put fencing and barricades across bridges that cross such obstructions. Seal off as many back streets as possible. Ideally you should have only one entrance to your area. If others are necessary, by all means use gates. If a potential aggressor comes across these fenced-off areas, and if he can't get inside to take a look, he might not want to attempt any aggression without knowing what to expect.

TACTICS

Your security measures must depend on how much land you have available. Contour and foliage also play an important part. Key points must be:

- Be aware of intruders' presence (alarms, patrols, guard dogs)
- Let them know you are aware of their presence (loudspeaker system, security lights)
- Don't let them know where you are (hide, never enter the open)
- Expose them, open them up, so all those insecurities will be exposed
- Scare them (security lights, alarms, hidden gimmicks)
- Confuse them
- Stop them, but don't kill them

Above all, be able to keep track of intruders' progress so you can counter their moves with something of your own. If every time they try an approach they are confronted with something new, it will demoralize them.

If you come across army flares that light up the area, aggressors might think the "Marines have landed." Be imaginative in your planning. Be capable of turning on lights at random throughout your farm area. What this is really all about is putting on a show—a show of force—psychological warfare. So don't kill them, scare them. If they are trying to kill you, you can legally kill them, but I hope you don't.

Use a speaker system to call out to aggressors. When you tell them to get out, don't be nice. Be aggressive yourself—even hostile. You must realize that they are there possibly to do you harm. Don't plead or beg or show any form of weakness. You have the upper hand—demand that they leave.

The bottom line is a matter of timing. If they break through your second fence and are running straight at you, you really don't have much time for fun and games. If they are lurking around the edge of your property you'll probably be able to scare them off, but draw your lines right—you can't make one mistake. If it's down to the last fifty yards, it's a matter of a warning shot and then you must act. If all else fails and you can't shoot, be able to get out fast. Be able to get out in two minutes or less. Keep your guns and valuables locked away where intruders can't use them.

Escape also requires planning. You must have a vehicle available and a passageway away from your aggressors. If they come in from the front, you must be able to get out through a back road. This road should go straight away from the house in two directions—hopefully toward a neighbor who can offer you refuge. Don't make the escape road completely straight. Set up a road that makes a sharp turn away from a ditch or other obstruction which might catch the aggressors unaware and disable them.

If you believe escape might be necessary, one of the first things to do is to get the children ready and in the car. Lock up valuables in preparation for the escape. It would be best to have an attached garage where the kids can climb into the car and wait. There they are out of the way and, hopefully, out of danger. When you are ready to run open the garage fast, at the last minute, and get out; don't go back under any circumstances! If people are after you they may charge in blindly if they see you running.

Chapter Six

ORGANIZATIONAL SECURITY

Many churches are now involved in food storage programs. They have really got the jump on most people by preparing to weather our coming hard times.

Latter-day Saints (the Mormons) have already given much thought to storage and how to protect their possessions. They have arranged storage places outside their churches or other dwellings known to belong to them. Being basically nonviolent, they must resort to hiding places rather than defensible positions.

I have heard of other organizations that are planning to minister during these times, giving food and support to the needy. These organizations have a very difficult job ahead of them. They must provide guidance and direction during the most difficult times our country might ever go through. In doing this they will open themselves up to a great deal of wrath, as stated in Luke 21:12: "But before this, they will lay hands on you and persecute you."

People who are not prepared will say, "Those rotten Christians have food and we don't have, so let's go get it."

What happens if you don't have food, or if you've hidden it away? Will others accept that you did not prepare or that you don't have a food allowance? I think not! The issue now is, What do we do? Do we fight? Do we run? Do we keep our food for only ourselves? It is a hard question.

The Bible charges us with the responsibility of providing for our family. Matthew 25:35-40 charges us with providing for our brothers, and those that don't will not receive their inheritance. King James Bible: "And the King shall answer and say unto them, Verily I say unto you, Inasmuch as ye have done it unto one of the least of these my brethren, ye have done it unto me. (Matthew 25:40.) This surely puts a burden on you, a burden the Lord will help you carry.

If we open up our homes and provisions to the mob, we wouldn't be performing as the Lord has commanded. We must provide for our family first, then provide for the "least of these my brethren" and then I'm sure the Lord wants you to provide for even the most sinful, perhaps witnessing to them on the way.

If you are to survive troubled times, many things must be prepared for. First, provide as much of a secured position as you intend to defend. Many of you will in no way shoot another person. If you are one of these you have to be in a position where you won't have to shoot. Second, provide alternatives to giving up all of your stores should that someone hold you hostage. A food cache system where you have your storage located in several places and hidden well can be very important. Third, never put all your eggs in one basket. Provide alternative life styles in the event you have to give up your home.

CHURCH SECURITY

I don't believe that church property is the place to make a stand. Short of putting one fence around the property and locks on the gates, anything further would put the people on the inside at a great disadvantage. Fortifications indicate that you have something to protect and that will mean someone will want what you are protecting. If a hostile group wants it and you are not prepared to protect it with hostility, it's theirs. This means that if a church family wants to help themselves they must do so without using their church as a storage depot.

ALTERNATIVE LIFE STYLE

A church organization can prepare alternative life styles for its family. This, of course, needs preplanning. If the church were to buy a farm with about two to five acres for every family they could probably set up an environment where they could survive quite well. This would require preplanning.

Find land in an out-of-the-way farming community where the climate is less than ideal. The population of such an area will be less and fewer people will seek it out in troubled times. It also means that the existing population is more self-reliant.

Property bought can be rented out to a local farmer to plant and harvest as long as you have the option of taking your share in produce rather than in money. You should further state in a contract that you will receive a percentage of the crop rather than a flat fee. A flat fee or rent in cash will be worthless if there is a 50 to 90 percent inflation. Long-term leases are out; you must be able to take back a percentage of the land at any time. The farmhouse and grounds can either be rented out to someone in your church who is interested in living in the area or to someone who can cope with your program. If you choose the right property, your congregation might want to spend their vacations there and maybe even make improvements.

The property should have a large parcel of improved agricultural land, but it must also have nonproductive land. This nonproductive land should be developed as time goes by. The first objective would be to turn this land into a campground, complete with sewers, water, and power. Set up your campsite with your future housing tract in mind. Place the camp in a defensible position, where your church family can move into trailers and other structures as time goes on. Build, in essence, a resort community with defensive security in mind. Choose an area that has as many natural obstructions as you can utilize; a closed-in canyon, the top of a hill, a setting as far back as possible from a main road.

As times get harder and people move in, they may want to build cabins or move in travel trailers or large expandable trailers. The expansion will probably occur gradually. The first families on the site must make provisions available for those who follow. If two families arrive, they must plan on feeding ten families. Families that come in must bring with them any livestock they can get, as well as any supplies of seed they can acquire. Further, when they come, they must be able to acquire farm equipment and building materials.

The ideal situation would be for the church to start stocking up now to be ready when the time comes. Trade your excesses for what your community might need. Keep in contact with them as you prepare.

The security of your community should follow the same guidelines as those for rural and residential security described in chapters two, four, and five. The only difference will be that your little town will have its own security force. The most capable people must be a part of this group: people capable of keeping their heads under pressure and capable of shooting only if their lives are in jeopardy. Choose your management well. This is no place for a person who can't make decisions.

As time goes on, walls, either concrete or wood, are going to be necessary. These walls should be built around your whole perimeter, with defensible positions planned. There must be at least fifty yards of clearing around your entire perimeter wall.

In making your decision to buy a farm, use this rough example: If your church has 250 families, with an average number of four people per family, there are 1,000 people to feed. If you buy a good basic diet of freeze-dried food for all these people, you will probably need to spend approximately $1,000 per person for a year's supply, or one million dollars in immediate cash outlay.

If you buy enough land to support these people, you probably need approximately two good acres per family, or 500 acres, for an average cost of less than one million dollars, the same as for a year's supply of food. But this million dollars can be financed on a month-to-month basis. Most land sales of this sort require 10 percent down and are financed over ten to twenty years. If you purchase a good piece of property and manage it well, the income from the farm production should help to support itself.

You will need to provide materials for your farm. These supplies should consist of at least basic building materials, seed, and some additional food storage. You should have farm animals on hand. The smaller ones such as chickens and rabbits will be most valuable. The larger they are the more difficult they will be to manage. If you have someone who is accustomed to handling cattle and other livestock, put them on the farm early.

When the need occurs, you will be looking at six months to three years that you will have to provide for your families. With the farm, the longer you stay the better you will be able to provide for them. A further advantage is that the property you acquire will increase in value far faster than any other property you could own.

THE FOOD CACHE

During a possible hostile situation such as I have been describing, it might be to your advantage to have small caches of food and provisions, so that if you are ever held captive you may be able to use these to bargain for your release. The use of underground storage, false walls and hidden cellars to use for your food caches will be of extreme value to you during these times.

Chapter Seven

RETAIL STORES

In this section I want to help the small retailer. Larger stores will be able to use other ways to protect themselves. They might even hire a security consultant.

My suggestions will be costly for the small retailer. In fact, if you are marginal now, you may not survive the financial troubles anyway. Prepare an alternate means of income that can keep you and your family afloat. Your preparedness now will equal your chances of survival later.

I'm not saying that there will be mass murder or mass anything else. But the Watts riots occurred because of social unrest. How unrestful will our whole population be when there is hyper inflation, food shortages, or a depression?

In this section we will deal with external as well as internal security measures. I want you to recognize that they are closely related. When there is less jeopardy for a cashier and less opportunity for external loss to occur there is more accountability for losses that do occur.

For instance, with one group of retailers I was able to prove that 50 percent of all armed robberies were phonies. What better way for a thief to help himself to several hundred dollars? He would steal the money, stash it, then call the police saying, "Help, I've been robbed." Who can question him? The police might doubt him, but unless the police can verify that the robbery was phoney, there is not much they can do. The only alternative is to eliminate the opportunity. It has to be impossible for a thief to stick a gun in a clerk's face and hold him hostage. We want to prevent shoplifting which will be an increasing problem in our future. Burglaries will occur more frequently. They will have to be contended with.

SECURITY OF THE FUTURE

The picture I will paint is for hard times, but there are those stores that are suffering so much that now is "hard times" for them. I will not deal with half measures. I am sure you as a retailer are already dealing with those. I want to concentrate on what may be minimum security in our future. Following is a customer visiting your store in 198?:

Jack Moss lives on Maple Street. Two blocks away is the Shoppers' Market. Since Jack has not had a car for over three months and only works part-time, he has to walk to Shoppers' Market when he needs any small item. When he arrives at the door of the Market he presses the doorbell. He can see inside. When the clerk waves, he waves back. Jack knows he will have to wait, because when he looked through the window he saw people in the store.

In about five minutes the door opens. A woman carrying a bag of groceries leaves. When the door opens, Jack holds it open so she can leave and he can enter. The outer door closes as he steps in. He is inside an inner room about six feet square. Another buzzer sounds, so Jack knows he can enter the electrically locked inner door. As he walks in, he can see Hank, the clerk, behind bulletproof glass. Jack knows exactly what he wants: five pounds of wheat, ten eight-penny nails, and a half dozen cigarettes. He picks these out and walks to the belt system. As the belt takes the merchandise into the clerk Jack goes to the paying window. The clerk asks him for twelve dollars even. He puts the money in a swivel tray. The clerk rocks it back so he can remove the money. The clerk counts the money and puts Jack's merchandise in a bag.

The clerk, Hank, takes the bag to a closet with a two-way door. He puts the bag in a container that opens to the six-foot inner room and closes the door. Jack has known Hank for several years, so they chat for a few minutes. Hank tells him of an experience he had the day before.

"Two guys came in and tried to hold me up." He chuckled. "One of them had a thirty-eight. He pointed it at me through the bulletproof glass. He told me to give him all the money. I said, 'Sorry fella, I can't do that, but if you leave now I won't call the police.' The first guy with the gun told the shorter one to crawl through the belted merchandise carrier to see if he could get a clear shot at me. Well, when he got halfway through, he yelled that there were bars in place and he couldn't see me at all. I thought the other guy was going to faint. By then I had pressed the alarm button and I knew that the police or security was on the way. I felt kind of sorry for the guy because he looked pretty desperate, but what else could I do? It's got to stop some way."

Jack asks, "Did the police come this time?"

Hank says, "Yes, and the guys didn't even go bananas when they found out they couldn't get out. They just sat and waited for the police. I even talked them into putting their guns on the merchandise belt so they wouldn't have them when the SWAT team came for them. Apparently they have heard how aggressive those guys are getting."

Jack asks "What are they doing with them?"

Hank says, "Well I guess they are put on those government work gangs; you know, the ones for Land Reclamation."

Jack says, "I'm sure glad I'm not that hard up. See you later."

Jack walks over to the inner door. A buzzer rings. He opens the door and walks into the entrance room. After the door closes, he knows he can take his bag out of the closet and go to the next door. He gets his bag and reaches for the next door. The buzzer rings again and he leaves the room.

As he walks out of the parking lot, two guys are standing out of sight of the store. One of them asks, "Hey buddy, what's that store like inside?"

Whether losses and problems will be that great at your store no one knows. I do know a lot of stores need this kind of security "NOW." Just ask someone in the more deprived areas what their losses are, and you will be shocked.

The store I described has three primary advantages.

First, by protecting the clerk from any form of aggression, robberies have been knocked down to nothing.

Second, when entry and exit of customers is controlled the shoplifter will think twice knowing he is closely scrutinized before leaving the store.

Third, if the number of customers who enter the store can be controlled the opportunity to steal will be substantially reduced.

Following is a detailed description of these measures as they would pertain to retail operations:

SECURITY BOOTH

The security booth is a portion of the store that will have to be completely self-contained. Restrooms, water, main power circuits, and air contitioning should be contained and controlled from within: restrooms so the clerk does not have to leave the secured area at any time; main power circuits so others outside cannot easily turn off the electricity; air conditioning and heat so the clerk will not be tempted to open doors to the outside. All power lines to the building should be underground and hidden.

The booth should have bulletproof glass throughout. The ability to observe the outside is extremely important, so make sure there is plenty of visibility. There should be two doors to the booth: one opening to the store, made from at least 1/8-inch heavy-gauge steel, encased in a steel frame; a second door of like design exiting to the outside toward the parking lot. Walls should be of concrete block, reinforced with steel, and filled with mortar.

The merchandise ramp should be constructed so the merchandise turns at least one corner before entering the booth. This ramp should have a set of bars before the corner that can be tripped into place with a lever.

The cash register should be placed so that it is in front of the window and facing the inside of the store. The amount rung up should be clearly visible with a sign at the register saying, "PAY THIS AMOUNT ONLY." (This creates an environment where failure to record sales is less likely to occur.) The cash window should be facing toward the store with a money exchange system that does not permit unwanted entrance of hazardous materials. (Someone could try to force the clerk out with tear gas or other substances.) The cash handler should be the type that has double doors, one on each side, so that when one is open the other will be closed and unable to be opened. Another such system would resemble a pipe. (See chapter on Gas Stations.)

The store can be of normal construction, but should be solidly built. It should be as fire retardant as possible, especially the roof. Iron bars should be in all windows to help prevent burglaries.

The store should have an alarm system that has direct tie-in with the local police department and at least one other location which could be a private security alarm board of a company official's home.

The alarm system should have at least the following:

1. Magnetic contacts on all doors and movable windows.
2. Foil strips on all windows. The foil should be glued to the glass eight inches from the frame around the entire window.
3. Concrete safes with a brittle metal grid. The grid should be put into the cement mold and the cement poured so as to have a covering of concrete at least one inch thick. This grid, when broken, will activate the alarm system.
4. All air conditioner openings with breakaway devices. If one is removed, the alarm will sound.
5. Ultrasonic or other area sensors present in the building because it is very difficult to protect all walls and ceilings from forced entry. A thief could bore a hole in any portion of the walls or ceiling without activating an alarm. The area sensor must announce a person's presence even though the perimeter alarm system has not been activated.
6. External alarm keys have been duplicated and by-passed on many occasions. Therefore, I would recommend an alarm put on a twenty-second delay so that, when you enter the building, you can deactivate the system with a key. Further, when you leave, you will have twenty seconds to get out after the alarm is activated.

The controlled exiting may give the retailers a problem. Our laws are now such that you must have fire exits even where exits don't normally exist. But when the time is right, that fire exit shouldn't be a part of what I described will be lockable. I'm sure the civil authorities will consent if your fire alarm system is hooked up to an automatic door opener. All anyone has to do then is start a fire and the doors are open. Work with your local government. They will probably work with you.

Chapter Eight

GAS STATIONS

Large multi-station companies as well as single-owner operators are going to be directly under the gun in this era. "Under the gun" is exactly what is going to happen. Gas stations are handling an ever-increasing amount of money—the most vulnerable money in our society today. Gas prices are over a dollar a gallon, and a lot of stations will pump more than 3500 gallons of gas daily. Over a weekend, some stations will handle over twenty-five thousand dollars. A lot of banks don't like to handle that much money now, much less in hard times.

Gas stations will be the number one targets of the future. The lack of security and screening programs has led to bleeding this business far in excess of what has been necessary. Hiring practices have been the number one problem in this industry.

DECOR

When it comes to any retail establishment, my Golden Rule—don't stand out as if you have something to protect—doesn't apply. Everyone will know you have the most money, the fewest employees to guard it, and often an employee most willing to hand over the money whether he protects his minimum-wage job or not. So advertise: "I am secure."

I went to a gas station once whose owners couldn't understand why it was always the victim of burglaries. The office was one of those very hot ones made of quarter-inch steel all around. It had bars on windows—on the inside. It was a formidable-looking building—from the inside. There was just one problem—from the outside it looked like a weak tin can with plywood patchwork. On the outside a piece of plywood covered the air conditioning hole. On the inside were metal bars. On the outside, covering a missing window, was a larger piece of plywood (used to tack up signs). On the inside again, heavy metal. It was literally patchwork paint, dirty, filled with holes.

Well, everyone and their grandmother thought this was easy pickings, so they tried. They drilled a hole in the ceiling and got in. They broke the lock off the restroom, cut a hole into the office and made their haul. Lots of others tried who didn't succeed. Later, the metal was patched with metal, the concrete was patched with concrete, new heavy metal doors were put in, everything was topped off with a new coat of paint, and things changed. That was a year ago and no more burglaries have occurred since. Total cost—four hundred and seventy-five dollars. Again, let's get back to Fort Knox—if it looks formidable, it is, but you will have to go much further than that.

SERVICE STATION CONSTRUCTION

That's right, build it over again. You have experimented with the cheaper ways for years. You have hired engineers to design your offices and pump grounds. Now let a security consultant design one.

The station office should be placed where it will look over the whole grounds, but close enough to the pumps to be convenient for customers. The office should be 20 by 20 feet square, at least. It should be built of concrete block reinforced with quarter-inch steel plating. Make your bunker well and make it almost look like one. Decorate it with tile or anything else you like but make it look solid. You should have an external door frame made from steel. The door should be steel, at least two one-quarter-inch plates. This door should face toward the islands and the street.

There should be at least four windows in the office. One window facing the front should be five feet wide and three feet high. On the left side, at the front edge, put a two-by-three-feet window and put another window on the right side at the front edge. You will also need a window facing the back of the station. All these windows will have to be bulletproof and tinted so that it will be hard to see in. Outside, on all the windows, will be iron bars placed four inches apart.

The roof should contain an operable air conditioner and heater. I've known many robberies to occur because the manager was either too hot or too cold when he had to count the money so that the door was left open and someone walked in with a gun.

Telephone and power lines should be placed underground and they should surface inside the builting.

Inside Functions

Inside the office, in the back, is a restroom, at least four by five feet, with a washbasin. No concrete is necessary on the inside: use pasteboard, or some other economical building material. Put the remaining window in the back of the building, on the back wall. The restroom should not take up the whole back wall, so there should be plenty of room.

In the corner where the cashier's window is, and off to one side, is a drop safe. This safe should be at least two feet by two feet by two and one-half feet high. There should be a metal chute about three-quarters of the way up, inserted into the safe container. This chute should be at least three feet long, and end up reasonably close to the cashier's window. The safe itself should be encased in a foot of concrete reinforced with steel. The drop-safe chute should have a rocker bar whereupon (once the chamber is opened to drop) there is no direct opening toward the bottom of the safe. The top of this concrete mass should contain a large safe head with the capability of a combination change. If the chute is sawed off at the edge of the concrete, the bottom of the safe would be at least three feet away at the chute so that the chute can't be made larger without breaking through the mass of concrete all the way to the safe itself.

Other than the solid construction of the building itself, the construction of the cashier's window is most important. Keep in mind a very important factor: you will have to be on a pre-pay system with a computer console at the cashier's station. The cashier's window may be set up in a bay window fashion as long as no shortcuts are taken with bulletproof glass and solid concrete construction.

The cashier's window is where design modifications may be necessary. If you sell oil, you may need a chute to deliver it to the customer. Even better is a container that can be used for cash or for any merchandise exchange.

Consider a piece of pipe—casehardened steel, 3/8-inch thick—lying on its side. It should have pivot points on each end so that the pipe can turn freely at those points. This pipe would be opened along its length so that two cans of oil could be placed inside. This pipe would be fitted into the window, in a frame, that would not allow a one-fourth-inch clearance. Add to the frame on the top a plate of like material to cover at least one-third of the pipe so that there would be no possibility of putting your hand through from the outside. Then stops should be added to the construction of the pipe so that the tray you have created can rock open to the clerk, and close to the clerk, and open to the customer.

Such a device would enable you to provide for all but bulk transfers of goods. Further, there must be a lever to forcibly close the canister holding it open to the outside. If the station requires large transfers of merchandise, a device such as is covered in the chapter on retail stores should be used. The following device is my own design but there are many devices on the market that will protect the clerk and still let the money and oil pass without jeopardy.

Now we have a completely secure office that no thief could ever gain access to, or have we?

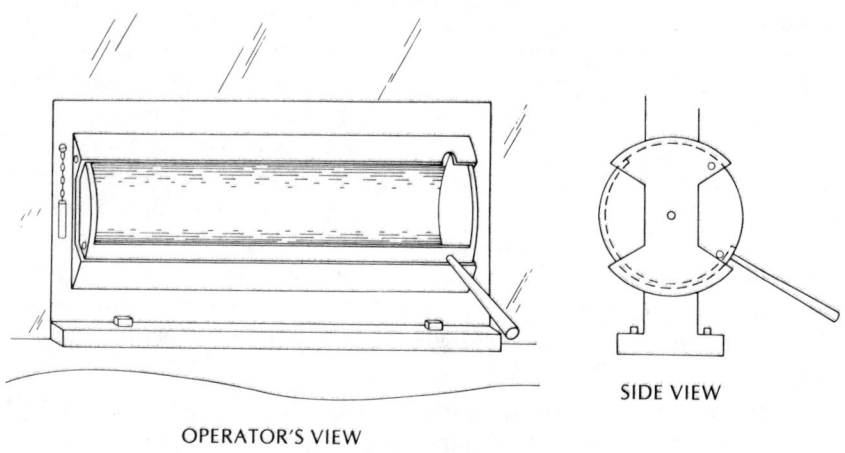

OPERATOR'S VIEW

CASH AND OIL HANDLER

COMPANY POLICY

Now we come to company policies. In my travels through various businesses, I have found that in every company there are those who steal so your policies have got to create accountability. The following policies are a must for the times that come:

Rule Number One: Never give supervisors the authority to count, handle, or touch station money.

Rule Number Two: Cash handling should go like this: the cashier drops the money and an armored car company picks up the money. The money is then taken to the bank. If losses occur at the station, a company auditor and one supervisor should be present. Until then, all hands off. Then the manager goes in the next day and watches the bank clerk count the money. *The clerk makes out the deposit slip* verified by the manager.

Rule Number Three: The manager should never handle money except on his own shift.

Rule Number Four: Attendant and manager may never leave the office once they enter until the end of the shift.

Rule Number Five: Never open the door to anyone except the manager or supervisor.

Rule Number Six: Never open or close or change shifts without having police or patrol protection.

Rule Number Seven: Never have more than one person handle money on a single shift.

The operation should go something like this for a two-shift station: The manager arrives at 6:00 a.m. and is greeted by a patrol car requested to be present at shift break. He unlocks the pumps and enters the office. (Once the manager is in the office, he must never leave until 2:00 p.m., when he quits for the day. He will operate his station only from the inside.) The manager turns on the pumps and whatever else is necessary, all from the inside. At noon the second shift cashier arrives. He can clean the station at this time or whatever is needed at the outside islands. When the manager thinks it's safe and security has arrived, he can enter the locked door to the office at around 1:00 p.m. The manager then turns over the shift to the cashier and gets ready for the armored car.

When the armored car arrives, it parks in front of the station door. The guards take the money, the manager's shift ends, and he leaves with armed protection. The cashier will have charge of the station from that point. He will not leave the office or open the door to anyone. He makes his drops timely because he doesn't have to move—just drops them down the chute next to him. At 8:00 or 10:00 p.m., when he is ready to leave, all money is down the chute. Lights are out, the patrol car has arrived, he locks up, turns on the alarms, and leaves.

This opens up possibilities. You can hire the handicapped since all that is needed is one hand and some intelligence. Legs are not necessary. He will be sitting down and only gets up to go to the restroom. Disadvantaged and handicapped people can now work for you where none could be considered before. Housewives who were afraid of dealing with the street environment and/or the handicapped can man your stations.

I am sure there is a station like this somewhere, but I haven't seen it yet. In the times we are talking about you won't exist without these minimums. Perhaps a lot of your stations can't exist without it now.

Perhaps the station in the future will have bank-type computers where the customer will actually deposit the money in the hands of the computer the customer will actually deposit the money in the computer which will then give change if the customer needs it.

Perhaps the company will use a chute that will drop the money inside the office into a glass box. Instead of the cashier handling money he will have a device to remotely move the money around in order to be counted. Then, if change is necessary, it will come from a change-making machine. In the meantime, the cashier pushes a lever and the money drops, without being touched, into a safe. Of course you might have to pay the bank a premium to count loose bills and coins, but it might be worth it.

Chapter Nine

INTERNAL THEFT PREVENTION AND DETECTION

YOU'VE MADE YOUR OWN BED

Since time began there have been thieves. In some cultures when a man was caught stealing his hand was cut off or he was hanged by his neck until dead. As man became more civilized, he became more humane; punishments began to more nearly fit the crime. Jail terms were handed out for theft or assault. Electrocution or gas was used for the murderer. Our pendulum was swinging from the most extreme to a more moderate, logical punishment. But as is the case with all pendulums, this one is still swinging. Now, thanks to our society, the criminal has everything going for him: there is more profit, less jeopardy, more opportunity and less opposition for the thief. "Who cares if you're a thief. Just don't steal from me!"

In our current society, according to every report I've read, eighty to ninety percent of all employees steal from their employers. It's not a matter of whether or not they have stolen; it's a matter of how much.

One reason for the ever-increasing crime problem is that many employers don't want to get involved. "I don't want the hassle. I'll fire him and he can go somewhere else," or "It will take too much time away from the business." The problem with this philosophy is that employees know about it. They are aware that if they get caught, they will only be fired. So why not try? They will only need to get another job. "Besides, I'm not a criminal. He owes it to me. I work harder than he thinks," or He owes me a raise." Few employees believe that an employer will prosecute if they are caught stealing. As a result, *no jeopardy.*

I want us to build a mental blockhouse. At the base is the history of our Founding Fathers and the principles and morals on which our society was built. The foundations are the Ten Commandments, the Bible, our Constitution, our national heroes, our work ethic, and our national allegiance.

Our society is in the process of pulling these foundations from under us. Christ's teachings are contrary to the new, more exciting sexual revolution. The work ethic has been replaced with a desire to get something for nothing.

INTERNAL THEFT PREVENTION AND DETECTION   95

Even though Christ may be "out" for some people they still feel a need to worship and to ask a divine power for something-for-nothing so they have turned to the devil, astrology, and—oh yes—to the U.S. Government. These alternatives often give them what they want without requiring them to be of good moral character.

The problems of our society are cutting deep holes in the flesh of our country. You, as an employer, are witnessing—and are being victimized by—one of the results of these attitudes: theft. You will go broke if you can't stop the thief. But you can hire the right people. You can control your employees and your losses. In the sections that follow, I will give you helpful hints and guidelines. In the times to come, if you don't prepare internally and externally for your problems, you may not survive.

APPLICANT SCREENING

In our society today there are many types of people who could be dangerous for an employer to hire. Among them are the most obvious: the drug addict, the thief, the abusive gambler, the abusive drinker. There are others, though, that can be dangerous as employees. Before we discuss these, let's define what constitutes a good employee.

He or she should have the following qualities:

- A desire to do a good job and succeed.
- Physically capable of doing the job.
- Mentally capable of doing the job.
- Stability. After he is trained, the employer must expect him to be around for a long time.
- He should not have any extreme problems that could distract from his performance, such as:
    drug addiction
    alcohol addiction
    gambling addiction
- Honesty. A person not accustomed to stealing to supplement his income.

Most employers judge their applicants by:

- Appearance.
- Enthusiasm.
- Employment application information.
- Apparent intelligence.

At this time I want to make several points:

1. An employee will put on an application what he thinks a potential employer wants to hear. An honest, stable applicant believes his potential employer wants to hear the truth. But the applicant who has problems

believes that a potential employer wants to hear all the good plus whatever else he can manufacture.

2. The most driven, aggressive or motivated person in our society today is the heroin addict. He not only wishes to succeed, he has got to succeed or suffer the consequences. As a result the addict's outward desire and enthusiasm can be deceptive.

3. Nine out of ten employers never give aptitude tests.

4. How many employees dress normally when they are trying to impress a potential employer?

Hiring techniques are the most arbitrary procedures in business today. The skills most employers use to make decisions are:

1. personal interview
2. Intuition
3. Employment application review
4. Intuition
5. Personal appearance
6. Intuition
7. Personality compatability

Sometimes they:

1. Verify application
2. Perform agility testing
3. Perform intelligence testing
4. Administer a physical examination
5. Administer a mental examination
6. And more intuition

Few employers are adept at screening applicants. Consequently they are open to a great deal of jeopardy. Further, they are handicapped. The Federal government has stepped in with laws and regulations that restrict an employer and limit his selection of employees.

Because of many lawsuits brought against employers by employees, an employer is most reluctant to even give a bad recommendation. If you know that an employee has stolen from you and if you give that employee a bad recommendation you may have to go to court to prove the accusation, spending thousands of dollars in the process. Consequently, more and more employers do not give out negative information. They will provide a date of hiring, a date left, and they will verify salaries. Sometimes they will even say the employee is eligible for rehire. Sometimes. Now, you're not only dealing with an imperfect skill but you are told that to discuss some issues is forbidden, and that the issues you can discuss most employers won't discuss because they fear for their own civil jeopardy. The problem is great and it gives a businessman one more handicap with which to contend.

All There Is Left

Although the problems are great they are not insurmountable. Our capitalistic system is very resilient. Whenever a problem enters the arena the American businessman seems to come up with a solution. The solutions I would like to offer have their own problems but since so many people are bent on destroying the American Capitalistic System these are probably among the best that can be suggested.

PERSONAL SCREENING OF THE JOB APPLICANT

Finding good applicants is a skill that takes many years to acquire. Some of that skill may be considered an art. To acquire it try the following hints:

1. Assign a monetary value to a good new employee. "I would be willing to pay $500 for a *good* employee." Whatever the value is that you assign remember that you will get what you have paid for. After you determine what a good new employee is worth, decide on a breakdown of the cost. I suggest the following as a starting point, but it will vary depending upon your own wants and needs:
    - Spend one-sixth of the cost on advertising for applicants.
    - Spend one-third on screening procedures: background investigations, polygraph examinations, physical examinations, and aptitude tests.
    - Spend one-half on training the new employee. Conduct structured classes or make it as simple as having the applicant spend several shifts with responsible supervision.

2. Decide on the media advertising that will best fill your need for new applicants:
    - Word of mouth
    - Classified ads: newspapers, throw-aways, *Wall Street Journal*
    - College placement offices
    - High school placement offices
    - Sign in business window
    - Unemployment offices
    - Federal or state job placement programs
    - Handicapped centers

3. Try to avoid the common pitfalls:
    - Hiring relatives can create factions within your company.
    - Hiring friends can also create factions.
    - Avoid panic hiring. You might hire a stand-by employee to fill your next full-time slot.
    - Avoid hiring the first person who comes through your door.

4. Decide on the procedures you will use to screen employees prior to your need for them. If you need employees *right now*, you are not going to be as objective about your procedures as you will be when the immediate need is not there. A typical procedure would be:
- Obtain an application and conduct a personal interview.
- Perform an intelligence test. (Observe the use of cash register, adding machine, computer terminal, or other abilitie's tests necessary.) You must be confident that the applicant's abilities are compatible with your needs.
- Verify all relevant information on the employment application.
- Use as many screening aids as you have decided you can afford: polygraph examinations, background investigation, medical examination, psychological examination.

If the applicant has cleared all of your screening efforts don't forget that compatibility is also a determining factor. This new employee may be a close part of at least one-third of your life.

APPLICATION FOR EMPLOYMENT

Every employer must have an application for employment that is designed to screen employees. Determine whether your application form is legal in your state. Several areas that must be covered are:

1. Always provide more space than is needed. If an applicant has had ten jobs in five years and you provide room for three or four, most applicants will just put down the best three or four employers. Those omitted may be those the applicant was fired from or had problems with.

2. Provide at least five spaces for residences, for the same reasons as above.

3. Use a verification process for each application you are considering. Verify all information to the best of your ability. (Be cautious when an applicant states that a company he worked for went out of business. Call the licensing department of that city and see if the company was actually doing business during that time. A lot of bad information can be covered up by one employer, now out of business.)

4. Obtain personal and family references. Verify their existence, addresses, and phone numbers. If problems arise such as a theft, you may be able to contact these people to locate your applicant.

USE THE PROFESSIONALS

Employers are often placed in a position where they cannot afford the time to adequately screen prospective employees. Besides, they may not have the abilities needed to investigate an applicant's past. In an era of specialization, this task can be handled by a more qualified person.

The Polygraph and the Applicant

The polygraph examination can be one of the most useful tools for an employer if it's used properly. The examination can yield information regarding theft from former employers, undetected crimes, narcotics addiction as well as gambling and alcohol problems. An examination can verify an employment application as well as yield additional relevant information not obtainable any other way. An employer must be cautious. There are certain pitfalls in using the polygraph. Some of them are:

1. Some states have no licensing laws for polygraph examiners. As a result there are examiners who are unqualified to administer these examinations.

2. In some states, such as Oregon, it is against the law to administer examinations to employees.

3. There are restrictive laws in other states, such as California, that state that you cannot demand or require that a person take a polygraph examination, nor can you dismiss a person as a result of the outcome. Even though this law is in effect, it is not damaging to a program provided the employer does not create an adversary environment.

4. If an applicant passes an examination conducted by an unqualified examiner, he, the applicant, may feel that he now has a license to steal because the examination does not work on him. With a competent examiner, this should hardly ever happen. Most qualified examiners have an accuracy rate of from ninety-five to ninety-eight percent.

5. Polygraph information disclosed by employers tends to make all employees feel very exposed. Confidentiality must be maintained.

There are immense advantages in the use of the polygraph examination when conducted by competent examiners.

1. Quite often the extreme individual will not take a polygraph examination.

2. The most devastating extremes are recognized for what they are prior to obtaining any position with the company.

3. Many admissions are acquired from those extreme individuals even prior to the examination.

4. The honest employees will benefit from the polygraph. They can feel confident that their fellow employees are not the extreme and consequently they will feel more comfortable with their jobs.

5. The examination can be completed within hours of the applicant's first contact with his employer.

6. Cost is generally one-tenth the cost of an investigation covering the same depth.

7. It sets the scene for the "constructive paranoia" that the employer has to maintain in order to decrease his losses. It lets the applicants recognize that the examination is not only a screening tool but that it will be used later to verify the applicants' continued honesty.

Many studies have determined that the polygraph will maintain a ninety-five percent accuracy ratio, at least, if the examiner is qualified. One of the most useful tools in determining whether the examiner is qualified is to determine what organizations he belongs to. The American Polygraph Association is a prime authority for credentials. Most states also have organizations such as The California Association of Polygraph Examiners. According to the American Polygraph Association, the following states now have licensing laws: Alabama, Arizona, Arkansas, California, Florida, Georgia, Illinois, Iowa, Kentucky, Maine, Massachusetts, Michigan, Mississippi, Nevada, New Mexico, North Carolina, North Dakota, Ohio, Oklahoma, Oregon, South Carolina, Tennessee, Texas, Utah, Vermont, Virginia. These are probably controlled so that an employee may get the best results.

Periodic Polygraph Examinations

Now and in the past, without the use of the polygraph, when an employer had a problem with a theft he usually used extreme and ineffective measures. Following a string of thefts, an employer often fired the last hired and worked back until the thievery stopped. The problem with this procedure was that a lot of innocent, good employees were the victims of a dishonest employee's actions. Further, the employer may not have fired the thief. The thief may have stopped stealing when things began to get too hot for him.

Secondly, if a group of employees had access to cash that came up missing, the employer would tend to doubt the honesty of that group. Even if he did not want to doubt them the money was missing.

Thirdly, if you were an honest employee, and with the extreme social pressure on you not to fink (narc, tattle) on your fellow employee, what would you do if your fellow employee was blatantly stealing from your employer? It has been my experience that over seventy-five percent of the time the good employee would move on to another job, leaving the thief to his plunder.

Fourth, like tends to attract like. If an employee is a thief, he wants to be around others who are thieves if only to lessen his own guilt and jeopardy. Further, a thief wants to make others become thieves so that he can feel more secure.

I want to point out the very positive points to be gained by using a qualified polygraph examiner. If he performs his task assuming that all who come before him are the honest, good employees, he may be able to save an employer many good and valuable employees.

A periodic polygraph examination should only be performed when an employer realizes that he has a loss problem. When he does, he must know that the thing of most value will be to recognize the honest employee. Second, he will know who has stolen and how much. A typical program must relate to the employer's inventory. When a substantial loss is recognized on an inventory the company should issue a memo stating that every employee will be asked to take a polygraph examination. They will then be asked to take another examination in two months. If the inventory is good, then no examination should be administered until the inventory shows a discrepancy.

Confront your employees as if they are the honest people you hope they are. Explain that the inventory shows a loss and that it must be dealt with the same as any other business matter, in a logical way. Explain that many things could have contributed to the loss such as shoplifting or an incorrect inventory but that you have established this policy for their benefit as well as to eliminate any chance of their being wrongly suspected, and that it is necessary to conduct the examination now in order to safeguard the honest employee. Explain that you are not willing to let the honest employees just fade away because there is theft in the company.

The polygraph is a valuable tool as long as you don't use it as a hammer to whip your employees into shape. If an employee steals, he must be fired. If an employee steals anything significant, he must be prosecuted to the full extent of the law. If you draw a line at, say, $100 cash before prosecution, thieves may steal $100 cash but no more. An uncertain policy will be stretched to the fullest extent so draw a line and use it.

Background Investigations

Background investigations conducted on prospective employees can accomplish many things. Most employers tend to use this service to do the basic research they, themselves, would normally do. An investigation would verify past employment, past addresses, driving record, and—if it applies—credit check and criminal records information.

It is becoming increasingly difficult to obtain information from external sources and, once obtained, the information tends to be incomplete. Further, the man-hours involved in this service can be long. Basically, the investigator is tied to what the other party wants to impart in the way of negative or positive information. The investigation has about a sixty percent chance of turning up the negative information necessary to determine whether or not an applicant is one of the extremes an employer might not want to hire. Most employers should use this procedure when the more economical means (the polygraph examination) is unavailable. Some companies may be bound by contract or laws that forbid the use of the polygraph. They may further feel, for whatever the reason they choose, that they would rather use the lesser information obtainable in the investigation.

Inventory Control

In the business community today are many small businesses that believe their situation does not warrant inventory controls. Further, some actually believe that it is impossible to inventory their stock. These are usually small retail operations with a lot of stock. The irony of this situation is that these businesses are apt to be the most vulnerable. They may have a very small staff—perhaps one person per shift. Employees are left on their own and often the employers are out of business and broke in a very short time. Every business should inventory their operation four to six times a year, minimum. Good inventories tell whether policies and procedures are adequate. An employer who is short three to five percent has a problem. As an employer, wouldn't it be nice to know that you have a problem? Wouldn't it be nice to stop it before it stops you?

Video Recorders

A new and exciting device is now available—the video tape recorder that can take a picture of clerk, register, time and customer all at once. These pictures are displayed on a television screen at the same time by using a split screen. The recorders usually run twenty-four hours taking pictures of all transactions. Further, voice recorders can be set to play with the recorder. An employer can sit down and review the prior evening's performance of his employees in a matter of minutes. This device can currently be leased for a very reasonable sum. It will accomplish many things but at least the following:

- The recorder will visually display any failures to record sales. The screen will display all merchandise as it is handed over as well as prices paid. This is an excellent deterrent.
- Shoplifters can be identified and photos made of the person actually stealing merchandise. I would like to see employers take snapshots of these people and post them in the store on a bulletin board. Can you imagine the effect that could have on any further theft?
- Armed robberies will be deterred. No one would want a photographic record of their crime.

I would suggest a monitor placed on the counter so that a customer can actually see his own image on the video. This will create that air of "Constructive Paranoia" which is so important in preventing crime.

Undercover Operatives

An undercover operation can be a very effective way to determine honesty, work performance, safety, attitude, etc., of your employees. It can also be one of the most dangerous investigations. When an investigator develops a personal rapport with his subjects, the subjects are more inclined to retaliate if the opportunity presents itself. An investigator usually takes on a position as an employee for one to four months and reports on what he observes as he goes through the workaday life as an employee. There are tremendous advantages in this operation. The major drawback is its cost, from four to six times a normal employee's salary.

Shopping Service

A shopping service consists of three or four investigators who travel from store to store testing for honesty, reliability, etc. This service is used for two distinct reasons. First, and most important, is to announce to employees that someone will be by to check on them. The shoppers will check on honesty, customer relations, cleanliness, etc. The prime use is for the employer to announce to his employees all good or bad reports. For the good employee, the employer will recognize his good performance and for the bad employee he is issuing a warning. Further, because the employee will not know who the shoppers are, he will begin to believe that a lot of his customers are shoppers and again create the "Constructive Paranoia." Secondly, the shopping service will, on occasion, be able to determine that an employee is stealing from the employer and should be able to testify in court. Keep in mind, though, that a shopping crew of three or four investigators will only be observing small segments of the employee's work performance and therefore will not be capable of determining the employee's complete honesty. They will only be giving an indication of honesty on maybe one one-thousandth of job performance.

APPENDIX A

Recommended Books on Financial Planning for Hard Times

When you read the writings of these authors I would like you to consider this: Almost every one of them has tried to lay down on paper what is tantamount to a prophetic view into the future. They have written about what they believe will be our future economic condition. In doing so they have observed cause and effect, action and reaction, but at the time they published their book they could only look upon a very serious economic environment and guess what the next moves would result from any one of ten thousand outside stimuli. As soon as they went to press the books were outdated: the "Fed" did this, the IMF did that. I think this may be one of the reasons why most of these writers tend to believe that hard times are coming sooner and harder than they are or have come. What they say all makes sense. I just think that in the interest of book writing they have chosen the "worst first" scenario. Perhaps what they predict will come upon us as they say, when they say, perhaps a little or a lot later. I do believe, though, that what they predict will happen in some form and maybe it's better to be two weeks too soon rather than a second too late.

Casey, Douglas R. *Crisis Investing.* New York: Stratford Press (distributed by Harper & Row), 1979.
> He calls it a depression but as near as I can tell we will get there the same way—through a massive inflation.

Durkin, Jim. *The Coming World Crisis.* Plainfield: Haven Books, A Division of Logos International, 1980.
> Economics from the Christian is really necessary for the Christian.

McKeever, Jim. *Christians Will Go Through the Tribulation.* Medford: Omega Publications, 1978.
> Mr. McKeever mixes economics and Christianity very well. He presents several good reasons why Christians can expect to have to go through the tribulation.

Pugsley, John A. *The Alpha Strategy.* Costa Mesa: The Common Sense Press, Inc., 1980.
> He goes the way of most authors but veers off stating that why not avoid the failing currency entirely and go straight into things. He tells you what things and why.

Ruff, Howard J. *Survive and Win in the Inflationary Eighties.* San Ramon: Target Publishers, 1981.

> One of the most famous authors on the subject, Ruff has sold more books and has a larger following than any other author. I have followed his newsletter and learned a great deal about economics for our future, as well as getting a good solid foundation of knowledge about the economics of today.

Ruff, Howard J. *How to Prosper During the Coming Bad Years.* New York: Warner Books, 1979.

> This is the book that put Howard Ruff on the map. He lets the reader in on all the illnesses our society seems to be suffering from and then tells us how to protect ourselves.

Skousen, Mark. *High Finance on a Low Budget.* Merryfield: 1981.

> Mark is really showing the little guy what to do, so maybe that's why no publisher published the book. At least I couldn't find mention of one. Everything in this book, almost, you can do for one hundred dollars. He gives the little guy places to go and people they can see. Everyone should read it. Write to: P.O. Box 611, Merryfield, Virginia 22116.

Smith, Jerome F. *The Coming Currency Collapse.* New York: Books in Focus, 1980.

> This book will show you what happened, how it happened and perhaps what's going to happen to the almighty dollar. I believe he is right on line.

APPENDIX B

Recommended Books on Physical Independence for Hard Times

As in any area of endeavor there is a right, a left and a middle-of-the-road view on how to do things. When an uninformed person hears the term "survive" he probably thinks of camouflage uniforms and automatic weapons.

When I hear the word "survival" I think of independence. When I prepare for hard times I think of hunting knowledge, gardening knowledge, wild, edible plants, trapping, bartering, storing of food and other necessities.

I would be very satisfied to be like the 60 percent of our population before the last great depression who were on small independent farms that stored up for the winter, grew and raised what they needed to eat, and seemed to be very capable of controlling their own lives and taking care of their own people.

But instead of 60 to 70 percent of the population on small farms and relatively independent, only 30 percent of the population live on farms today and of those very few grow their own food. They only grow crops.

My objective then, and my recommendation, is to become as independent as possible. Learn to garden, to barter, and make some plans for what you believe will be your future.

Benson, Ragnar. *Survival Poaching.* Boulder: Paladin Press, 1980.

> I dislike the name, don't like some of the language, and it seems as if I had just read a confession that would hold up in a court of law, BUT it is one great book that can tell you how to trap anything that moves.

Dickey, Ester. *Passport to Survival.* Salt Lake City: Bookcraft, Inc., 1969.

> For anyone who has ever considered a basic food storage plan: wheat, salt, honey, and powdered milk. She makes the project almost likeable.

Hertzberg, Ruth. *Putting Food By.* Brattleborough: The Stephen Green Press, 1975.

> What's the sense in having food if you can't take care of it? This book will show you canning, freezing, drying, root cellaring, curing, sprouting and preserving meats and much more.

Nelson, Louise E. *Project Readiness: A Guide to Family Emergency Preparedness.* Bountiful: Horizon Publishers, 1974.

> Here is the encyclopedia of emergency preparedness. It covers food preservation, storing water, pest control, recipes, lighting, cooking, sanitation, etc. One of the best basic books in the field.

Seymour, John. *The Guide to Self-Sufficiency.* New York: Popular Mechanics Books, 1976.

> A complete how-to book for the homesteader, better than his prior book, "Farming for Self-Sufficiency."

Stoner, Carol Hupping. *Stocking Up.* Emmaus: Rondal Press, 1977.

> How to freeze, can, dry, pickle, jam or juice it. And there is another section on meats, and nuts, and sprouts. If I were to weigh this book with "Putting Food By" this one would win, but I am very sure that they both do the job quite well. I bought them both and I am happy I did.

INDEX

A

Active defense, 58, 64
Active patrol, 59
Alarm system, 32-39
   choosing alarm company, 39
   central station, 36
   farms, 78
   inputs, 32
   power supply, 32
   procedures, 58
   sensors, 33-34
   switch, supervised, 32
   two zones, 32
Alternative life style, 82
Apartment complexes, 69
   closed system, 70
   fencing, 69
Application for employment, 98
Applicant screening, 95
Area sensors, 34
Audible panic circuit, alarm, 32
Audio system, 35, 37
Automatic alarm, 33
   reset alarm, 32
   security lighting, 16
   telephone dialer, 32, 36, 39
Automobile panel, alarm, 32
Auxiliary power, alarm, 32

B

Background investigations, 101
Barbed wire, 29, 62, 72, 77
Barrel bolt or lock hasp, 18, 19
Baseboard vault, 41
Belted merchandise carrier, 86
Block walls, 29
Brittle metal grid, 88
Bulletproof glass, 63, 86, 87
   gas station, 90
Bunker, gas station, 90

C

Call boxes, 72
Cam lock, 44

Case-hardened steel, 19, 25
Cash handler, 88
Castle, 71
Cedar chest in the floor, 42
Central station, 36
Chain lock, 19
Choosing an alarm, 38
Church security, 82
Closed circuit TV, 72
Closed security system, 61
   apartments, 69
   hard times, 61
CN Gas, 53
Combat skills, personal, 53
Combination door lock, 25
Communications, 63, 75
Company policy, gas stations, 92
Constructive paranoia, 59
   polygraph, 100
   video recorders, 102
   shopping service, 103
Control panel alarm, 32
Controlled exiting, retain, 88
Cooperative construction, 29
Crime avoidance, 15, 49
CS gas, 53

D

Deadbolt, 19
Dialer, direct, 37
Dog runs, 30
   guard, 30
Doors, 17
   external, 19
   garage, 19
   locks, 19, 24-25
   metal, 19
   sliding glass, 20
   drop-safe, 91

E

Education of others in hard times, 67
Electromagnetic fields (see Microwave), 34
Electromagnetic sensor, 72

Employment application, 95
Entry delay, 32
Eyebolt lock, 22
  double-hung windows, 27

F

Farm
  alarm systems, 78
  communication, 75
  community road blocks, 78
  escape from the farm, 80
  gates, 77
  home construction, 78
  perimeter security, 76
  security, 71
  tactics, 79
  ultimate security, 72
  wall defense positions, 77
Fencing, 29
  apartment, 69
  farm, 73, 76
Foil, 33
  retail, 88
Food cache, 84

G

Garage locks, 19, 24
Gas, CN and CS, 53
Gas stations, 89-92
  decor, 89
  construction, 90
  company policy, 92
Gates, farm, 77
  hard times, 58, 61
Glass doors, 19
Guard dogs, 30
Guard house, 58, 63
Guards, 61
Guns, 54

H

Hard times security, 57
  active defense, 64
  active patrol, 59
  closed security system, 61, 70
  communications, 63
  education of others, 67
  gates, 61, 77
  guard house, 63
  observation points, 65
  porches, 67
  steering committee, 57
  timing for hard times, 68
  windows, 65
Hasp, 18-19, 24
Heat detectors, 32
Hedges, 29

Hiding places, 40-44
Hinge, non-removable pins, 18
Hinged windows, 28
Home construction, farm, 78
Horns, 64

I

Input sensors, 33
Intercom, 17-18, 64, 78
Internal theft prevention & detection, 94-103
  applicant screening, 95, 99
  application for employment, 98
  background investigations, 101
  inventory control, 102
  personal screening, 97
  shopping service, 103
  undercover operatives, 102
Inventory control, 102

K

Key control, 26
Keyless locks, 25

L

Latchlock, 19
Lighting, 16, 79
  alarms, 46
Lived-in home while away, 16
Local alarms, 37
Loudspeaker system, 78-79

M

Magnetic contact switches, 33
  retail, 88
Martial law, 59
Merchandise ramp, 86-87
Metal grating, 20
Microwave sensors, 34, 38
Microphones, 78

N

Neighborhood security, 44
  passive watch, 45
  alarm procedures, 46
Nonremovable bolts, 19
Normally open/closed, 33

O

Observation points, 65, 66
One-inch deadbolt, 20, 25
Open circuit, 33
Organizational security, 81

P

Padlocks, 24
Panic switches, 33

INDEX

Passive watch, neighborhood, 45
Pedestrian door, garage, 19
Perimeter, security, 76
Periodic polygraph examinations, 100
Personal protection, 48
Personal screening of applicant, 97
Photo-electric devices, 36, 72
Physical fitness, 53
Police department alarm, 36
Police in hard times, 58
Polygraph and applicant, 99
Porches in hard times, 67
Power source, alarm, 32
Pressure-sensitive sensors, 34
Professional defenses, 52
Proprietary alarm, 37

R

Razor wire, 29, 72
Residential security, 14
Retail stores, security, 85
Roadblocks, farm, 78
Roofing, 30
Rural or farm security, 71

S

Safe, gas station, 91
Security, booth, retail store, 87
  cam lock, 44
  screen, 19
Self-confidence, 52
Sensors, alarm, 33-34
  light, 16
Shock sensors, 34
Shopping service, 103
Shrubs, 29
Shutters, 66
Sliding glass doors, 20
  metal plate, 22-23
Sliding windows, 28
Smoke detectors, 32
Sound for the home, 17
Sound waves (see Area sensors), 34

Speakers, 78
Strike plate, 20-21
Steel pin security locks, 27
Steering committee, 44
Supervised keyswitch, 32
SWAT team, 86
Swivel tray, 86

T

Timers, lighting, 16
  sound, 17
Timing for hard times, 68
Transmitters, battery-operated, 34
Trees, 29
Two-zone, 32

U

Ultimate security, 72
Ultrasonic sensor (see Area sensors), 34, 38
  retail, 88
Undercover operatives, 102
Underwriters Laboratories (UL), 38

V

Vibration sensors, 34
Video recorders, 102
Viewers, wide-angle, 18
Vigilantes, 44

W

Wall defense positions, farm, 77
Watch dog, 30
Wide-angle viewers, 18
Windows, 26, 65
  double-hung, 27
  encasement, 66
  for hard times, 65
Wrought-iron doors, 19, 65
  windows, 19

Z

Zone, 32